The Vital Nail

Bruce Samways

Dedication
for Peggy

Always my inspiration

A sketch of Peggy by Bruce made when he was at camp in Aden

Acknowledgements

I am very grateful to my brother, Kenneth, for his skill in rendering reproducible my faded prints. *Bruce 1986*

*****

3

Preface

My father, Bruce Samways, died in 1987 after a short battle with pancreatic cancer. Before he died I promised to get his book published. The manuscript has been in his worn leather briefcase under my stairs.

Despite a few attempts to put it into a format that could be considered for publication it had remained an unfinished project. The discovery of iPad dictation and the enforced lockdown of the summer of Covid 19 meant that the time normally spent on other family and community orientated tasks could be devoted to fulfilling this promise.

When travel was curtailed because of the pandemic, typing this book took me on an imaginary journey with my father around the British Isles, including family favourite haunts in Dorset and Devon. Then I was transported to unknown Egypt and Aden and to the beautiful country of Ceylon, which I have been fortunate to visit.

My father always instilled a sense of adventure into our happy family life. The journey taken to reach publication has been another rewarding adventure with the love and support of my family and friends.

My thanks must go to John King for his great assistance in editing the manuscript and to Philip Judkins for his help and encouragement to publish. Many friends and family kindly offered to read the drafts and gave valuable feedback, especially Beric, Carl, Richard, Dorothy,Tricia and Brenda. I am indebted to Anita and Rob who have produced a splendid cover design.

Rosemary Keele (granddaughter no.3) 2020

Author's Note

Over half a century has passed since the events of which I write were played out against the backdrop of World War II. The mighty and evil forces of both Germany and Japan, in their turn, so very nearly succeeded in conquering the free world and the balance of success or failure often depends on quite small factors.

Countless books, from accurate and historical studies and detailed personal accounts through to fiction have covered almost every aspect of the conflict, so why should I think there is room for one more?

I can plead three reasons, if not excuses. First, although much has been recorded of the scientific contributions to the war effort, I am not aware of a published personal account of the workings of the radar system.

Second, I just happened to be 'on the spot' (and only just in time) at perhaps, the most critical moment of the whole war.

Third, I would like my children and grandchildren to have a contemporary account of our way of life in those perilous times before they were born; when lovers were parted for years on end and letters could take three months; when an adult meat ration for a whole week was the amount you could buy for 4p. So, if much of this account is personal, even nostalgic, it is all true.

Although the climax of my story came on 9th April,1942, on a beach in Ceylon, the train of events that took me there began years before. For the sake of completeness, I have covered the decade from 1936 to 1946, (years which saw many changes in my life), and which spanned the time from the emergence of Hitler, as a dictator, to the final defeat of Japan with the atomic bombing of Hiroshima and Nagasaki.

B. Samways   1986

Historical Notes

7 December 1941

Admiral Nagumo, commanding a force of six aircraft carriers, two battleships and two cruisers, treacherously attacked Pearl Harbour with his massed aircraft, sinking five US battleships and destroying 188 American aircraft. His own losses were 29 planes out of some 400 high-level bombers, dive bombers, torpedo aircraft and fighters. So, started the great Japanese adventure which brought America into the war and which ended at Hiroshima and Nagasaki.

15 February 1942

In just five weeks, Japanese land forces had swept through Malaya and taken Singapore, inflicting the greatest ever defeat on Great Britain, and opening the way to the mighty Indian Ocean.

Admiral Nagumo was ready to strike westwards. The focal point for the Allied defence of the Indian Ocean, of India itself and of the seas all the way to the Suez, was clearly the island of Ceylon. This was to be the Admiral Nagumo's target, as he set forth with a fleet comprising five aircraft carriers and four battleships.

31 March 1942

The British Eastern Fleet, who had suffered glorious losses in the attempts to defend Singapore, withdrew from Ceylon, some of its ships retreating all the way to Africa.

5 April 1942

Admiral Nagumo flew off 130 aircraft, at dawn, which arrived, unopposed, over Colombo. Just as at Pearl Harbour, he achieved total tactical surprise and did much damage: but the main British fleet had gone.

9 April 1942

Admiral Nagumo, now cruising some 200 miles to the east of the island. Flew off his third (and as it proved, his last) mass attack on its way to the greatest natural harbour and Naval Base of Trincomalee.

This time, to his surprise, his formations of bombers were intercepted by Royal Air Force Hurricanes, whilst still thirty miles out at sea. He had, for the first time, encountered effective enemy radar, with which none of his ships was fitted, and he knew at once, that the balance of air power had shifted against him. What he did not know was just how pitifully thin our defences were, nor that our handful of Hurricanes were being guided by just one solitary line of flickering green light: a few days earlier, even that had been lacking.

Admiral Nagumo withdrew his task force all the way to Japan, and no such force again entered the Indian Ocean.

6 July 1944

Admiral Nagumo committed suicide.

The Vital Nail

Chapter 1

Early Days 1936–1938

> For want of a nail ...
> The shoe was lost.
> For want of a shoe ...
> The horse was lost.
> For want of a horse ...
> The rider was lost.
> For want of a rider ...
> The battle was lost.
> For want of a battle ...
> The Crown was lost.
> For want of a nail ...[1]

The crown, in 1936, was safely on the head of King George V, and England felt a secure place to live in—the centre of the British Empire, surrounded by a sea ruled by the Royal Navy, under blue skies controlled by the Royal Air Force—or so it seemed.

To me, then seventeen years old, war meant stories told by uncles of the Great War, a thing which happened years ago (although I was born just seven weeks before it ended). I knew of course that Hitler and Mussolini seemed now to be emerging as dictators; even that they had ideas of increasing their authority beyond their natural frontiers—but that was unlikely to affect us. We were British.

---

[1] This proverb, initially a nursery rhyme, was quoted by Benjamin Franklin.

9

Much more important, in the summer of 1936, was the exciting beginning of a new life for our family. My father, who had managed the same pharmacy for 24 years—the North Watford branch of Timothy Whites—gave up his job and the secure £12 a week it brought in, sold our house for £800 and moved us to Gillingham in rural Dorset, to partner his eldest brother in the original family pharmacy. This was indeed a changed way of life for us all, bringing much hard work and happiness, and also a dreamed-of luxury, a motor car. ALD 312 was an Austin 7 saloon, in perfect order, two years old, and it cost us just £50 against the new price of £100 for the model.

We all worked. The pharmacy had a news agency, so the day began before 6 am with a drive to the railway station for the papers. We were open until 7 pm on most weekdays, until 8 pm on Fridays, until 9 pm every Saturday and until midnight on Christmas Eve.

Meal times were constantly interrupted by the bell, as my father was the only qualified pharmacist on the premises to supervise the poisons cupboard—and after the shop door was finally shut many a late prescription was brought to the house door. I filled in for any absentees at any task I could be trusted to do, unpacking stock, delivering newspapers, manning the cash desk—especially the latter.

The shop assistants did not handle money: they wrote out a ticket for the sum owing (keeping a carbon copy in the counter book) which the customer took to the desk to pay. The cashier (me) then had to write the sum on the till roll, where it showed through the slot provided and then spiked the ticket on a spike file before opening the drawer. As you opened the drawer, a bell went PING! and the roll notched forward to leave a space for the next entry. At the end of the day Father had to add up all the counter book copies, add up the till roll entries, see that they agreed and then count the money to that matching the till roll. Then the money was put in a tin box and hidden behind a loose board in the dispensary until it could be banked the next day.

10

The Axis powers in 1936 were flexing their muscles with a view to world domination but were no doubt hopeful that they would not need to fight. The rest of the world was curiously indifferent, although a few far-sighted men were doing their best to see that we were prepared. Among these, Robert Watson-Watt found that enough electro-magnetic radiation was reflected from an aircraft in flight to suggest a possible way of detecting aircraft beyond the range of sight and sound, and I, quite unknowingly, was being led inevitably towards my share in that venture; for as a promising science scholar I was to return to school at Watford to try to win a Cambridge scholarship and become a physicist.

Watford Grammar School had a good academic record, and it was proud of its technical status as a public school (as I recall, this status depended partly on the Head being a member of the Headmasters Conference, but rather more on the fact that we had an annual cricket fixture with the MCC). Anyway, the academic status was undeniably high, and it was my duty to gain one of the two customary Oxbridge open scholarships or exhibitions in the year.

So I was packed off back to school, to live in lodgings as a lonely 17-year-old. My landlady was a motherly soul who fed me lavishly on full board and did all my laundry (including rugby kit twice a week) for just £1-5-0d weekly. That autumn, in the Science Sixth, I had to forgo Saturday morning rugby and instead, for three solitary hours, sit by myself in a classroom doing an (old) Cambridge paper under examination conditions—one week of physics, the next chemistry, the next mathematics and so on. These papers would be critically marked for my enlightenment by Monday morning.

Naturally, although I undeniably learned a great deal through this system, I did not relish losing out on the rugby, so I usually managed to get an afternoon game for the Old Boys B Team.

The morning of December 11 found me standing on the down platform of Watford Junction station. If I could select one memory to epitomise life in the 1930s and '40s of that century; it would be of standing on a platform waiting for a steam train. It is not just that often one had to wait far beyond the proper time according to the timetable, but rather these departures (when the train eventually puffed and hissed its way in) marked a sudden, and seemingly complete, transfer from one phase of life to an unknown future.

One moment you were standing in a place you knew well enough, talking perhaps to family or friends who had come to see you off; then the monster took you on board and rattled you off to some unfamiliar place. After a few seconds of waving from the open window, smelling the warm steam and getting a hot cinder in your eye, you sat back with a feeling of excitement tinged with apprehension: one phase of your life had just ended (would it ever return?) and now, what did the future hold?

And so railway departures stick in the memory to this day, as though they were guillotine blades chopping one's life into slices. Always, before the blow fell there was an agonising wait, precious minutes which you wanted to fill with happy memories and brilliant conversation; but all too often you could think of nothing to say.

That December morning l had no-one to see me off. It was the chance overhearing of another traveller's remark "I never thought he'd abdicate" which told me that Edward VIII was no longer my King. This was not to be the last time when I was to overhear, by chance, news that would change the course of history, but it was the first time, in my 18 years, when it suddenly struck me that the Great British Empire might not, after all, continue on its serene way forever.

Perhaps, after all, the German threat would grow; perhaps some at least of Hitler's tanks were not made of cardboard; perhaps I would find myself in the army one day.

I boarded the train and shared a compartment with a kindly old gentleman, to whom I confided that I was off to Cambridge to sit an open scholarship, but that I had no hope of success. He gave me much encouragement which I badly needed, for a solid week of examinations in a strange town, living in strange lodgings was a daunting prospect. For three hours each morning and each afternoon I pitted my brains against the examiners, and it was a hopeful sign when, on the Friday, I was bidden to stay on for a Saturday morning interview.

This proved to be with an old—an extremely old—professor who was, it seemed, a chemist. He spent a long time explaining to me that his great interest was the history of chemistry, which was not exactly good news since history was certainly not my strong point, neither did I rate my chemistry very highly. However, he seemed to be content to do the talking, so I listened politely and bided my time.

After half an hour, he asked me his one and only question: "When did Lavoisier do his work on oxygen?"

"About 1780, Sir," I said promptly.

"And how did you know that?" he asked, clearly warming to a fellow historian.

I thought it best to be truthful. "The only two dates I know are 1066 and 1789, and as Lavoisier was intimately connected with the Revolution, in fact he had his head chopped off, he must have done his work a bit before, Sir."

That concluded the interview. I had no idea whether I had done myself a service by answering so glibly and took the train back to Watford without much confidence that I should see Cambridge ever again.

***

A few days later, suitcase in hand, I set off for Dorset and Christmas holidays—by underground to Waterloo and by the old faithful 6 pm train, first stop, Salisbury, which would, I knew, get me into Gillingham at 8.18 pm. However many times I did that journey, it was always a thrill to leave Salisbury and feel that the journey was almost over now we were on the "stopping" part of the trip. "Wilton, Denton, Semley and Gillingham" had a Betjeman-like lilt to it, even in those days when steam trains were commonplace and railway nostalgia had not been invented.

After Semley the train travelled fast down the slope from Salisbury Plain to the Blackmore Vale, and I hung out of the window for a glimpse of Duncliffe Hill in the moonlight just to convince myself that I really was home. What I did not know then was that the next few days were to produce two events, both of which would profoundly influence my future.

The first was the arrival of a telegram saying, "Congratulations on Major Open Scholarship at Queen's College." Without this, of course, no university education would have been possible, so suddenly my future appeared to be mapped out for me: an academic scientist I would become. But I had no thought then that this turn of events was destined to lead me to a commission in the Royal Air Force and into a secret development which would have a profound effect on the outcome of the next war.

The other event was that I went to a tea party. The proprietor of the local cinema had a son of my age and two younger daughters, so this party covered "teenagers". It seems a little strange today, but before the war an 18-year-old, as I then was, was still considered to be just a schoolboy. There were no discos and teenage drinking was unthought of. Apart from anything else, one had no money for frivolities and a shilling cinema seat with a tuppenny ice cream in the interval—why, that was the height of extravagance. So off I went, like any other schoolchild, to the party.

I can remember very vividly walking up the road to Peasemarsh (a corruption of Peace March, the scene of the truce after an Anglo-Saxon battle at the neighbouring "Slaughter Gate") and espying in front of me a young girl in a party frock and white ankle socks. She was accompanied by her mother, who duly delivered her to the front door and then departed. I followed into the farmhouse lounge, and there was Miss Party-frock, looking at me with blue, blue eyes and a welcoming smile.

14

And that was that—love at first sight, and mutual too. She was then 13-and-a-half years old.

The next eight years would see us constantly separated but always together in spirit—and so we are to this day, half a century later.

I soon learned that she had a most convenient elder brother who worked in their father's printing office. He joined the party after work at 6 pm and so became a very useful, though totally unsuspecting, ally in my courtship. But that had to wait, for I was due to go back to school.

I had two more terms to complete at Watford Grammar School. Although I had already passed my Higher School Certificate, it was very necessary to sit this examination all over again, to gain higher marks, for on this result depended a county scholarship and without this extra money Cambridge would not be possible.

In the end, I recall, I collected a Dorset County Senior Scholarship of £80 a year, and a School Governor's Exhibition of £100, being £40 in the first year and £30 for each of the second and third years. My Open Scholarship was worth £100 a year, so I thus had a grand total of £640 which paid all my fees and expenses for three full academic years. By living carefully, I actually came out with a tiny profit.

These two years I was, it seemed, always coming and going, by train in winter and bicycle in summer. The terms, both at school and at university, were largely devoted to study while the vacations, without exception, were devoted to anything but study and I scarcely opened a book in Dorsetshire.

But the holidays and vacations were not just a round of sport and pleasure, although there were some opportunities for swimming and tennis. Rather, my days were well occupied in unpaid work, alternating between two locations at opposite ends of the town. For most of the opening hours of the pharmacy I was involved in helping as I have described; this passed the mornings and afternoons.

15

Immediately after tea, however (unfailingly at 4.30, served by our housemaid), I escaped up the road to the Blackmore Press to the clatter of the typecasting machines and the swish of the printing presses. Here I was again in a family business environment where everyone worked—mother, father, sons, daughter, even grandfather—all doing what they could, and I was no exception. I soon learned the secondary skills such as collating, stitching, guillotining and packing, and many hours of such work were my passport to a second tea at 6 pm and to snatched moments in the back kitchen with the master printer's daughter.

It is impossible to look back on those days without a reference to the highlight of the summer, the annual Agricultural Show. Whatever happened, the Show catalogue just had to be printed and delivered on time, and the night before the opening day saw all hands hard at work until midnight.

***

Early in October 1937 I took the train for Waterloo, the tube to Liverpool Street and again to Cambridge. As an Open Scholar I was privileged to "live in" in my first year, and I secured almost the cheapest room in Queens', under the eaves at the top of P staircase. This was on the fourth storey of Fisher Building, and those six flights of stone steps did wonders for me—not only did they increase the distance I could kick a rugby ball quite remarkably, but they also proved to be valuable memory training: one soon learned not to leave anything behind in one's room and have to climb all the way back to fetch it!

The way of life of a "young gentleman" who "kept rooms" at Cambridge was still based on the tradition of domestic service which had survived the First World War but which then had only less than two more years before disappearing forever. My rooms comprised a separate bedroom, a living room with a desk, dining table, cupboard, armchairs, open coal fire and a gas ring. A sack of coal was delivered weekly to a bunker in the staircase and from this my scuttle was filled regularly by my "bed maker".

Some colleges used only male servants or "gyps", but the Queens' tradition was for female servants who came daily to clean, tidy, wash up and make beds: hence they were known as "bedders". According to University Statute such women had to be *nec juvenile nec pulchra,* and certainly I never saw one either young enough or beautiful enough to tempt a young man.

The suite of rooms was completed by a separate gyp room just about big enough to contain a sink and running water. Toilets and baths were across the court in another building, so the gyp room and its sink were universally used for toilet purposes—at least by those of us who lived on the upper floors. One of the bedder's functions was to deliver daily a loaf of bread and a pint of milk—commons—and it was a recognised perk of their job that they could (and they did) remove for their own consumption any remaining from the day before. On this food, supplemented by what we bought in like cereals and sausages, we lived for breakfast, lunch and tea.

Dinner every night was in the Hall, and attendance was compulsory: summoned by the college bell, one had to be in place, on time, ready to stand in silence while the dons filed in to take their places at High Table. Then, all still standing, the duty scholar read the grace in Latin: *BENEDIC, DOMINE, NOS ET DONA TUA! QUAE DE LARGITATE TUA SUMUS ET CONCEDE UT ILLIS SALUBRITER NUTRITI TIBI DEBITUM OBSEQUIEM PRAESTARE VALEAMUS, PER CHRISTUM DOMINUM NOSTRUM.*

As an Open Scholar I had to perform this duty for a week every term, standing on the edge of the dais bearing the High Table.

Dinner in Hall and sport were about the only truly college-based activities, for lectures and laboratories were all university centred. Life in college for a first-year scholar was a lonely existence, and my few friends came mostly from those with whom I played rugby. They, of course, had to live out in lodgings, so breakfast and lunch were solitary meals for the most part.

My living-in rooms were, naturally, very useful to my friends to repair to after dinner for coffee, before cycling back to their lodgings to be locked in at 10 pm by their landladies. In college, too, 10 pm was lock-up time. After that time, one could be admitted by the porter, with your name taken for reporting to your tutor, on payment of a gate fine of sixpence, but failure to be in by 11 pm meant trouble.

Most undergraduates therefore would climb in after 11 pm, and there were a number of recognised routes of differing severity. I used a route over a double row of spikes from Queens' Lane, leading to the back of a bicycle shed. This was a well-known route but also well-known to the college porters, who were liable to lie in wait in the cycle shed after 11 pm. For me, sixpence was a lot of money, so I often climbed in between 10 and 11 pm just to save the gate fine, when the night porter would be still in his lodge, taking the names of my richer friends.

Cambridge, in that autumn of 1937, was a lonely place. Despite my 19 years, I was still a schoolboy at heart and adapted but slowly to the greater freedom of a university. I attended lectures and laboratories assiduously, spending much time in the Cavendish Laboratory. I fondly believed that I was training to be an academic scientist, whereas in truth my future was already being shaped to meet the needs of the war.

The very building in which I worked had seen the pioneering research leading to the splitting of the atom and in other ways which, in retrospect, seem all too plain now. I was already being inched along a conveyor belt which would ultimately discharge me into World War II as cannon fodder. It was well that it was so: the Battle of Waterloo might have been won on the playing fields of Eton, but this next war was to be won on the benchtops of British and American Universities.

Even back in 1937, many of us in the Cavendish knew of the awesome prospects of nuclear power and knew that some aspects of the work in the building were not for discussion. I was too junior ever to take part in that decade of work that led, in 1945, to the sudden ending of the war through the destruction of Hiroshima and Nagasaki. Instead, I was all unwittingly headed for a role in the cast of the other great technological miracle of the time, RDF.

Although I had some inkling of atomic energy, I was blissfully ignorant of RDF, as were all but a handful of scientists and senior officers of the services. Not for another two years would I hear those magic letters, and even then, they were never to be spoken! Even if they were ever heard in public, they were designed to obscure their true significance, for they stood for Radio Direction Finding, and there was nothing new or secret about that. The words "Radiolocation" or the Americanism Radar (RAdio Direction finding And Ranging) were not to be spoken until many years later, and the vital secret was heavily guarded.

But I anticipate, and we must go back to the Cavendish and 1937, where my course of studies, based mainly on classical physics of "heat, light and sound", "properties of matter" and "electricity and magnetism" was already being infiltrated by atomic theory and electronics, as science nudged itself along the paths leading to World War II.

Certain little incidents remain indelibly on the mind of those days: of hearing, blaring from a wireless set at someone's open window, the screaming harangue from Adolf Hitler to a Nuremberg Rally, followed by the roar of applause from the Nazi faithful; of the overhearing, in the crowd at a University rugby match, the conversation, "What will you do when the war starts?" "I shall become a name on one of those brass plates in the local church" (I have often wondered if that flippant reply was prophetic); of learning, with some amazement, that one of my friends in the OTC was still being taught the cavalry charge, sabre in hand, having been assured that horses still had their place in modern battle; of a certain supervisor (to whom I paid three guineas a term for personal tuition) complaining that he was not allowed to go into certain parts of the laboratory "because he was not British".

We saw, too, the pacifist movement among students, pathetic and misguided, which culminated in that celebrated Oxford Union debate which carried a motion "This house will not fight for King and Country" and whose stupidity is said finally to have convinced Hitler that Britain would not fight and could be incorporated into the Third Reich as easily as Austria.

Rag Day at Cambridge was always on November 11, and all proceeds went to the Earl Haig Fund. At Queens' we mounted a barricade on Silver Street Bridge and claimed a toll from every passing motorist. This was heavily supported by the vast majority of students, but even then there was the pacifist fringe who tried to sell white poppies "in aid of peace". Many of those young men at Oxford did, in the event, both fight and die for their country; maybe they were, all unwittingly, the final factor which brought about the war and so caused their own deaths.

Through those years of 1937 and '38 the clouds of war thickened on the horizon, both nationally and on the level of the individual. We all thought the storm was about to break when, at the last moment Neville Chamberlain flew back from Munich waving his bit of paper, and we all cheered. I remember my father running down the beach at Exmouth, where we were enjoying a late holiday, and shouting, "Hitler's climbed down!"

Even then, as I joined in the general euphoria, I can recall having some lingering doubts.

Chapter 2

1939: War Looms

One can never know, and no one ever will know now, what were the true inner thoughts of Neville Chamberlain, with his "Peace in our time" on his lips and his signed chit from Hitler in his fingers. With savage hindsight, most of the nation condemned him as a gullible old man, well-meaning but easily duped. Others, deeper thinking, say that he knew we were totally unprepared in 1938 and that he sacrificed his good name in order to buy another year of time to rearm for the coming struggle.

It is probable that, materially, Germany increased her strength more than the Allies during the last year of peace, but in the matter of public opinion and mental preparation for the fight we made great strides, as more and more it became clear, even to young men like us at Cambridge, that before long we should have to fight.

That last peacetime summer saw me, duly be-gowned, sitting and sweating in the Market Hall in the middle of Cambridge, as I ploughed my way through the written papers of part one of the Natural Sciences Tripos.

On other days, in the laboratories, we had six-hour non-stop practical examinations (no gowns, bring your own sandwiches) in Chemistry and Physics. This was a culmination of two years' effort and of vital importance. Natural Sciences (with three whole subjects and optional extra half subjects such as Mathematics), alone among Triposes, was the only one to offer an honours degree for one part only, and this could be spread over the three years' residence. I had crammed it all into two years so that I could be free to study Part II Physics for the whole of my third year—if I had one, that was. Indeed, there was some doubt as the signs of war grew more numerous.

In April a limited form of National Service was introduced, and I was just in the age bracket, so at the first minute of the opening hour on the appointed day, I walked into the labour exchange to register, as required by law. Young men of my age were to be given basic training, and I recall my amazement at reading that, because of the shortage of uniforms, we were to be given a "walking out" uniform comprising slacks and a sports coat. How on Earth, I wondered, were we to be equipped for war if the nation could not even clothe its soldiers properly?

Registration, in my case, was soon followed by a direction to complete my studies, so in the first week of June I turned my back on the last of peacetime Cambridge and set off by pushbike on the first stage of the 150-mile trek home to Dorset. I cycled for the very good reason that it saved the train fare and I thought nothing of it, calling on my brother in Ware for a meal and overnighting at my old lodgings in Watford.

Next morning, early, I took the lower road to Rickmansworth, through Denham to Windsor, and so down the A303 across Salisbury Plain. The hundred miles of this stage took 10 hours, with no stops for meals; a bottle of water and a couple of dry bread rolls provided sustenance. Some of the hills on the plain were daunting, but it was best to keep going, even if it meant standing on the pedals and zigzagging up the worst inclines. I neither walked nor even dismounted, from door to door, and scarcely was I home to greet my parents than I was off on foot, up the High Street to Blackmore Vale House to greet my sweetheart— unofficially, of course, for she was still a schoolgirl and I was just a friend of the family.

Three days later came a telegram from Norman Hughes, my closest college friend. It read simply, "Bruce, Ted, Norman, all first," so I, together with Norman and Edward Rollinson, had secured first class honours. All we had to do now was to keep three more terms' residence and be of good conduct, and honours degrees were ours, even if we failed Part II.

But I had no thoughts of the academic life when in Dorset and devoted my days to the family business and my evening to a clandestine courtship. The Blackmore Press occupied an old school room in the grounds of Blackmore Vale House, which was blessed with a sizeable garden containing several mature trees, and there was scarcely any distinction between working in the house, working in the garden and working in the print shop. Indeed, it was quite common to find the machines running, all by themselves, while father and sons, and mother and daughter too, were occupied on other tasks. If a machine tripped out or came to the end of its stack of paper, the change in the noise soon brought someone to get it going again.

I soon joined this happy working family environment, paying my way by helping in both work and play—cutting the grass, lopping trees, working the guillotine or the stitcher, sharing meals—and literally camping in the garden, for Bertram and I were keen on the outdoor life and shared a tent and a campfire in the orchard.

That summer vacation brought me my first paid job. A local solicitor, Clerk to the Magistrates, found that all his clerical staff were due to go to Territorial Army training camp, and he engaged me for four weeks to do all his office work for the total sum of £3. I answered the door, manned the telephone switchboard, taught myself to type, typed wills and contracts——one mistake and you started all over again: splendid discipline!—and every Friday collected the five shillings each due from the local unmarried fathers under court paternity awards, which I duly paid out on Saturday mornings to the unmarried mothers as they queued up at the side door with their perambulators. It was quite an education for a young man.

***

Already, that July and August, it was becoming apparent that war was coming. It was no longer a question of "if" but of "when", and sadly the nation began to make preparation. The mass bombing of towns like Guernica during the Spanish Civil War led the government to expect the same thing to happen to us as soon as hostilities started, and two civilian measures were proposed for immediate implementation on the outbreak of war.

These were for a total blackout and for the evacuation of children from city to rural areas. The first of these gave me plenty of work that summer, for we had a large three-storey house and seven shop windows to make lightproof. Happily, we had available large quantities of stout, opaque, brown kraft paper, saved from the wrappings of bundles of newsprint and other goods, so I bought large quantities of one-inch and three-quarter-inch battens and made half-jointed frames to fit every window in the building. I covered these frames with brown kraft and arranged fixings so that they could be put up and taken down each night and morning.

(After the war, when all things were scarce, this timber was re-used by me for many purposes, among which were the construction of a high chair, a cot stand and a clothes horse for our first child—a twentieth century version of beating swords into ploughshares.)

For the evacuation scheme, Gillingham was to be a reception area and lists were made of all available accommodation, but our house was exempt in view of my father's essential occupation as a pharmacist, so we did not have to plan for the sudden arrival in our home of strange city children. I was enrolled, however, as a member of the reception team, to serve as a driver for distributing children to outlying farms, should the need arise, in our faithful Austin 7.

It is difficult to analyse the thoughts of a young man during this period of growing likelihood of a war, but certainly I had no fears or doubts whatsoever, either for myself or the nation, at that time. I was young, confident and in love, so any war would be just another small obstacle to overcome on my way forward to future happiness.

Indeed, a larger and more immediate obstacle lay in the way—the very proper and protective attitude which Peggy's parents took over their schoolgirl daughter in the presence of a young Cambridge undergraduate. On one occasion I was even to receive the classical Victorian words, "Go, and never darken my doors again!" but I bobbed up as usual the next day as though nothing had happened.

No amount of parental disapproval could stop our arranging other clandestine meetings and on July 1, 1939, but nine weeks before the outbreak of war, we pledged our eternal love. I was a near-penniless student and she was a 16-year-old schoolgirl, but it seemed to be the most natural and sensible thing to agree that our future lay together. We were right.

Meanwhile, the world around us rushed headlong into war, and the invasion of Poland by German forces caused the British government to take emergency measures. On the morning of September 1 trainloads of young school children, grouped by school forms under their own teachers, left London for unknown destinations, each child bearing a tie-on label with name and school. These groups duly arrived at their schools-in-exile throughout the West Country, and Gillingham, Dorset, received its quota.

I did my share in assigning these bewildered evacuees to their billets until the end of the morning, when there were just two grubby little boys left. "Where are these going?" I asked.

"To Mrs Brickell at Newbury."

"I'm just going there—I'll take them," I volunteered. So, on foot, with five-year old Joey in one hand and three-year old Charlie in the other, I walked up the High Street and knocked on the door of Blackmore Vale House. Peggy opened it.

"I've brought you your evacuees."

"You're joking." But it was no joke, and the two miserable, damp, cockney kids (their father was an East End docker) were taken to the back kitchen, stood up on the table and stripped.

Their discarded clothing went into the fire and they were bathed and re-clothed from the sparse contents of their own battered suitcase and by borrowing from local mothers until new clothes could be made on the hand sewing machine.

The outbreak of war two days later came as something of an anti-climax, as though the country's emotions had been expended over the parting of children from parents, and we all knew that war was now inevitable. Inevitably, too, one's mind was concentrated on the personal aspects: what would it mean to me?

Some thought of this must have gone through my mind on that Sunday morning, September 3, as I walked up the High Street, but I cannot recall any doubt about the eventual outcome of the war, nor any fear at all for my personal safety. My immediate plans were just to be with Peggy as the announcement was made, and then to see what happened next. I suppose I knew instinctively that this would be different from the last one; that I did not need to go at once and sign up as a private soldier as my uncles had done in 1914; and that my services would be used for my scientific skill in some way. (I had not taken seriously the advice given to me by Peggy's father a few days before, which was to join the navy, on the grounds that "you always had a bed to sleep in because you took it around with you on a ship". This curious logic seems to have sprung from his experiences in the First World War in the army.)

So it was in a carefree mood that I turned into the ever-open gateway of Blackmore Vale House, perhaps a trifle excited at the prospect of unknown adventures to come, but certainly not apprehensive. In those days "the wireless" was the focal point of every household, as is "the telly" today, so we switched it on together in the otherwise deserted front room and sat together in father's own armchair as Neville Chamberlain's words came sombrely from the loudspeaker ..." ... No such assurances ... a state of WAR ... "

At this precise moment the room door opened, and Peggy's father came in. I shall never know whether his prime concern was to hear the news or to protect his daughter's innocence, but we stayed on unmoving in our embrace and he, wise father (remembering perhaps from his own youth the lovers' partings which war was bringing to us) stood silently and listened with us. And so, unspokenly, our love became official at the precise moment when the world was plunged into World War II. There is no doubt at all which was the more important to Peggy and me.

**

It is impossible to avoid some deviation from strict chronology in recounting the events of those days, and it was only some time later, after I had joined the secret war of the RDF, that I knew the inside story of the next few hours. All we knew then, from the wireless, was that Chamberlain's announcement was followed soon after by an air raid warning, but that no bombs seem to have been dropped on us.

As I was later to learn, one of the chain of radar stations had a faulty sensing switch. It must be explained that in those early stations the transmitter aerials were intended to floodlight a wide area out to sea with short pulses of high-energy radio waves, but that some of this energy spilled out behind the station overland. The echo signal from an aircraft was received in fact on two receiver aerials at right angles one to the other, and the relative strengths of the two receptions were measured, to give the angle of the bearing of the aircraft. (Its distance was determined by timing the delay of the echo, so that, knowing angle and distance, it's precise location could be plotted.)

Now there was only one slight problem: a single angle measuring device like this could not distinguish between a signal coming from, say, northeast, and one coming from the reciprocal bearing of southwest. To overcome this, the operator could use an extra reflector (by operating his sensing switch) which would show a stronger signal for the true direction and a weaker signal for a spurious reciprocal reception from inland.

What happened on that morning of September 3 was that a friendly aircraft inland was wrongly reported as approaching from across the North Sea. Moreover, as fighters were sent up to intercept they showed up as even more hostiles coming in.

So we waited for the bombs to drop, and none came. The country rapidly settled down into the "phoney war" and even a dangerous feeling of complacency. Many of the evacuees drifted home and theatres were allowed to reopen. British troops moved to France and established themselves at bases well behind the security of the Maginot Line. For me, there were just four more weeks of vacation before the new term, the last four weeks of a way of life which would never return.

During these weeks I acquired my basic military training by watching the Territorial Army troops who drilled

28

daily in the square opposite our pharmacy and who were billeted in the building opposite. I observed how officers conducted parades and how to present arms; and I marvelled at how little really productive effort there was. Why should I, for example, still be on holiday instead of frantically digging trenches or learning how to stick bayonets into Germans? It seemed that we were again preparing to fight the last war as the infantry learned their basic drill before my eyes and my mother joined the Red Cross.

We also took in, as paying guests, the wives of two of the Territorial Army officers from Plymouth so that they could be near their husbands for a few weeks before their inevitable departure to France and to death or glory. One of these officers, learning that 24 September was my 21st birthday, produced a bottle of wine to drink my health. I never saw him again.

Early in October I returned to Cambridge and found it a curious mixture of "business as usual" "and "don't you know there is a war on?" Gone were individual rooms, and I slept on a camp bed in doubled-up accommodation, shared with a second-year student, Geoffrey Hollis. Lectures and sport were unaltered, or so it seemed, but I took turns in fire watching and learned to run out a flat hose under the guidance of the head porter, ex-CPO Johncock.

More meals were served in Hall and lectures were shared with evacuees from London University, but superficially little had changed. An extra course of lectures, however, seemed to have appeared in our Part II Physics Tripos, and it was hinted to us that it might help our degrees if we went to them. This was on the mysteries of wireless telegraphy.

I dutifully followed this and picked up smatterings of knowledge about capacitors and inductances and tuned circuits, and the theories of the diode and triode valve. There was no practical work, and I was very much at sea compared with some of my friends who were amateur radio enthusiasts and had built their own receivers. I did my best to learn the basic facts, mostly without fully understanding them, and this was to be valuable in helping me to flannel my way through difficulties later in the war—with a combination of a little basic knowledge, some intuition and a lot of bluff.

Somewhat to our surprise, there were no air raids that autumn as the days shortened and winter took over. I remember thinking, rather conceitedly, that so many budding scientists concentrated in a small area (easily located on a moonlit night by following the river) ought to be a prime target for a bombing raid—but nothing happened.

Cambridgeshire was full of aircrew trainees. An abiding memory of that autumn is the sight of columns of marching, singing, cheerful young sergeant pilots swinging through the college backs, bound for they knew not what. At that time I had absolutely no thought that I, too, was soon to be one of the boys in blue, but already fate had it all worked out for my future, and in the last few days of term I was one of a select few physicists who was bidden to a meeting addressed by Professor Sir Lawrence Bragg. He could not tell us anything except that we were invited to give up our Christmas vacation to do secret work for the Air Ministry. Would we volunteer?

According to theory, vacations were to be used for study, especially in one's third year, but this was our professor speaking and there was just a tiny hint that if we gave up our time to this mysterious project, perhaps our degree prospects would not suffer. I never gave the matter a second thought and volunteered on the spot.

I had scarcely reached home in Dorset, for what was supposed to be the Christmas vacation, when on December 12 a telegram arrived which read: "REPORT TO SUPT AMRE TECHNICAL COLLEGE DUNDEE."

It was only later that I learned that the capital letters AMRE stood for the Ministry Research Establishment, and later still before I knew that this was the code name for the research establishment devoted to the use of radio for detecting aircraft. In my innocence I thought that I had to report to a Mr AMRE, and Dundee seemed as far away as

30

the North Pole for one who had never been farther north than Nottingham.

It was therefore in a spirit of high adventure that I packed a suitcase, said goodbye to my parents, walked to the railway station and bought a ticket to Dundee. Two hours after receiving the telegram I was leaning out of the carriage window as, yet once more, a steam train hauled me away from Gillingham and my hearth and home. At Salisbury I got out. I knew that with a through ticket one could break one's journey at will.

Chapter 3

Christmas in Scotland

I left my bag at the Salisbury station and set off on foot through the darkening, blacked-out streets to an address near the cathedral. Here, I knew, my Peggy was staying in a Salisbury school, as she had to retake her school certificate. She was lodging with the mother of another pupil for the week. This astonished lady (who clearly felt her responsibility for the moral welfare of the schoolgirl invested to her care) had scarcely time to protest before I announced that I was taking Peggy to the cinema and would bring her back safely.

Off we went into the darkness, Peggy clinging to my arm. Whatever repercussions might follow, we had a few brief hours before the last train to London would snatch me away. All is fair in love and war, so we felt justified on both counts.

I think the film was *Wuthering Heights*, although my memory of the screen was no more detailed then than it is now. It was enough to be sitting and holding hands in the darkness and warmth; that was the main reason for the sale of cinema tickets in our young generation and we asked for nothing more until the end of the performance.

Peggy insisted on seeing me off from the station, so that it was past 10 o'clock before she arrived back at her lodgings to the relief of her distraught hostess. As for me, I reached London just in time for a hurried trip from terminus to terminus and boarded the midnight train for the north.

Nineteen hours later, sleepless and hungry, I reached Dundee, found the technical college and explained myself to a rather bewildered night duty officer, who sensibly directed me to a small local hotel, the Queens, with orders to report back in the morning.

This was the first time I had ever stayed in a hotel, and I recall the comfort and luxury it provided in the shape of a cup of Ovaltine and a rubber hot water bottle. I needed little time before falling asleep, still not knowing why I was there at all.

Next morning, back at the technical college, I first had to sign a pledge under the Official Secrets Act and was then told to sit in the library and read through a *very* secret document. This typescript, in a temporary binder, was apparently all that was then on record concerning the magic and mysterious world of RDF.

These three letters, themselves so deadly secret that they were not to be written or spoken in public, stood for Radio Direction Finding which itself was a cover phrase, innocuous enough. The determination of a direction from which radio waves came could be done easily with a rotatable, directional aerial, and this had been known for years. What was hidden behind the code letters was the new and exciting principle that if you sent out a very short pulse of very intense and powerful radio waves, these would bounce back off an aeroplane in the sky with sufficient strength to be detected by a high-powered receiver.

Further, if you timed accurately the fraction of a second for the signal to go out and back, you could work out how far away the aeroplane was; and finally, by measuring the points of the compass from which the return echo came, you could pinpoint the aircraft in space. (It would be several years before the American word radar would be coined.)

I felt an immense thrill at being party to the secret and went on to read the outline of the operational system known as "the chain" and comprising some half-dozen chain stations or CHs which were spread along the east coast. At the time these were built, the shortest wavelength available was around 15 to 20 metres, which caused severe limitations to the system. A concentrated beam of radiation can be produced only from a radiator many times wider than the wavelength, so that even with the use of 360 foot high masts, it was possible to have a radiator only three or four wavelengths across.

Consequently, the radiation took the form of a very wide-angle floodlight which covered the seaward area in front of each station. There was one such station for about every 50 miles of the east coast.

I checked quickly through the calculations which showed that it was indeed feasible to radiate enough energy, over such a vast area of sky, to give an echo which could be detected, after much amplification, by a radio receiver and displayed on a cathode ray tube.

My reading was soon interrupted, and I was told I was to go to Anstruther to work on the only CHL station in the country. I would find out what it was when I got there, and "there" was the Commercial Hotel, Anstruther, where I would report to Sub Lieutenant Evans RNVR.

Anstruther was on the north shore of the Firth of Forth near its outer extremity and so, suitcase in hand, I crossed the Tay by the steam ferry and made my way by bus to Anstruther, where I took a room, which I could ill afford, in the Commercial Hotel: I had to sleep somewhere, but I was rapidly running out of money. So far, there was no sight of the £5 a week which I was supposed to be paid as a temporary civil servant.

Evans was a pleasant young graduate who should have been doing research in botany but was called up at the outbreak and diverted by the navy into this new-fangled technology. He took me off to show me his command, by way of a tuppenny bus ride up the coast, and at a certain bend in the road he had to call the conductor to stop the bus and we then set off on foot across two fields where, on the edge of a low rocky cliff, surrounded by a barbed wire fence, was a collection of wooden huts. Over two of these were built low wooden gantries, and on these gantries were, apparently, two large hen-coops made of chicken wire.

This impossible contraption was the only installation in the country capable of giving any warning of approaching enemy aircraft below about 2000 feet, and it is a tribute to the wisdom of the Air Ministry that it was in operation at all, even in such a makeshift and undeveloped state.

As I was to learn later, the more conventional and senior services, the Royal Navy and the Army, were fond of long periods of proper training before battle, but this policy needed a co-operative enemy who was prepared to wait until we called "Ready". In the RAF we were in the front line the whole time. It was a fortunate thing that the senior RAF officers in 1939 were those same go-ahead young firebrands who had seized the chance of joining the new service in 1918 to break away from the more staid admirals and generals of their young days.

(I am conscious that this is too sweeping a generalisation: the RAF too had its misfits, just as the army and a navy had many gallant and daring commanders. But still, undeniably, there was a much greater display of initiative and a much greater willingness to be tolerant of the mistakes of amateur enthusiasts like me in the Royal Air Force than in the other services.)

***

It is worth describing in a little detail this first operational CHL station at Anstruther. CHL stood for Chain Home Low-flying and it operated on the then almost unthinkably short wavelength of 1.5 metres. This meant that you could stack radiating dipoles, tuned to this wavelength, into an array five radiators wide and four high, in a rectangle measuring some 30 feet by 15 feet. Place a chicken wire reflector behind it, feed power to all radiators in phase, and you got it—not exactly a searchlight beam but at least a beam like that from a lighthouse, extending only a few degrees on either side of its line of shoot.

Now, place the whole thing on a searchlight turntable and you could sweep from side to side. The higher you could place this above sea level, the better it was for indicating low-flying aircraft.

Now you need another similar array for a receiver aerial and, providing the two are pointing in the same direction at the same time, you will pick up an echo from the low-flying enemy.

The means of traversing our receiver beam seawards from coast to coast was delightfully simple: a long bicycle chain from the turntable came down through a hole in the roof of the hut, and an operator sat, turning the pedals by hand, back and forth, back and forth, while he watched the cathode tube for echoes. In the transmitter hut, another operator with an identical bicycle chain and pedals had to rotate his transmitter so that it pointed always in the same direction as the receiver aerial. To assist him in this, a system of master and slave self-synchronous "selsyn" motors provided pointers on dials to show the directions in which the two aerials were pointing. All the operator had to do was to keep the pointers parallel—and keep from falling asleep.

That December 1939, three months into the war, the only low-flying cover for the whole British Isles depended on two men turning bicycle chains by hand.

There was on site a small detachment of Scottish Territorials, assigned to guard duties around the clock. The technical personnel (mixed service and civilian) were mostly billeted out, and I found a spare bed in a little cabin, intended for the site commander. I arranged to sleep here, going down to Anstruther for my meals and vacating my room at the inn, strictly as an economy measure.

This arrangement gave me more time on the station after dark, when we might have expected enemy action, and I spent many such hours studying the operation of the system and taking turn as an operator. Thus it came about that early one morning I was the only senior person on site to receive an important and totally unexpected visitor. A neatly dressed, elderly civilian was seen approaching the gate on

36

foot, and as his pass was in order he was admitted by the guard and I found myself entertaining the father of RDF himself, none other than Mr (later of course to become Sir) Robert Watson-Watt, who had come to look at the first of his CHL stations.

The business of gaining admission to these secret stations was taken very seriously, and my own temporary pass, signed by Sub Lieutenant Evans, had to be replaced by a proper permit. This meant a trip to RAF Station Leuchars to be photographed, and this was my first visit to an operational aerodrome. Already the RAF was beginning to put its fingers on my collar, for it was clearly the most attractive of the Services for an individualist like me.

Armed with my new pass, I arrived back at the roadside, well after dark, on a moonless night and set off down the track across the fields, deliberately making a noise as I walked. A challenge rang out, unmistakably, "Halt! Who goes thurr?" although the accent was so broad that I froze into immobility more from the tone and rhythm of the shout than from understanding the words. Quite unmistakable, too, was the click of the bolt as a round went into the breech.

"Friend!" I shouted.

Back came a mouthful of Gaelic, not one word of which could I understand: it could have been anything from "Advance, friend an' be recognised" to "Tak another step and I will blow ye head off." Now here was a dilemma, for I knew that a few nights earlier a sentry had shot dead a totally innocent sheep which had not acted correctly when challenged.

I screamed "Friend!" again, and back from the darkness came a similar torrent of highland accent. I thought I had better do something, not just stand there, so I held my new pass out at arm's length (sideways) and walked slowly forward, with the vague hope that the pass was likely to be the first thing that came into sight and that the sentry was not such a bad shot that he would be three feet off target at a range of three yards.

A few more steps in ominous silence, and then the beam from a torch lit up my pass. I halted. The balance of probability seemed to be that the next two words were "Pass, friend," so I slowly, slowly, crept forward and was admitted through the barbed wire.

This was the time of the so-called phoney war, at least in Europe, but just before Christmas the wireless brought us news of the Battle of the River Plate and the British triumph over the *Graf Spee*, and that Russia was taking advantage of "our" war to invade Finland. German air activity was confined to reconnaissance and we plotted our first "hostile" approaching the Firth, but it retreated without crossing the coast.

We came to our first Christmas of the war and my first away from home. To me it was a working day, or there was nothing better to do than watch in the operation room in case the enemy chose the holiday to mount an air raid while we British were, presumably, asleep from the effects of too much food and drink. Our CO, who was visited by his fiancée over the holiday, was naturally glad that I volunteered to stand in for him—not that I could do much except telephone him for help if things went wrong.

Happily, nothing did.

Chapter 4

1940: The Real War

The New Year brought several weeks of sharp frost and the rationing of meat, bacon, butter and sugar, for German U-boats were sinking many of our ships in the North Sea and the Atlantic approaches, but apart from the black-out, domestic life in Britain returned almost to normal.

On January 10 I left Anstruther, taking the local train and crossing the Forth Bridge in daylight, to reach Edinburgh with some hours to waste before the night train southwards. As always, the solution to the problem of cold, hunger and hours to wait lay in the local cinema where, for half a crown, one could sit in reasonable warmth, eat baked beans on toast in the restaurant and come out with a few coppers in change.

There followed another night sitting up in a third class railway compartment, another early-morning crossing of London, luggage in hand, another wait at Waterloo for the morning train westwards, another unheralded arrival at Gillingham station (for we did not, in those days, think of making a trunk call by telephone, except in the greatest emergency, because of the cost), another walk down the High Street, bag in hand, to another surprised and delighted welcome home—for just three days, and then off again on another steam train, back to Waterloo, across to Liverpool Street, up to Cambridge and to the coldest January for some years.

The skating was splendid, and safe, because once the ground was frozen the locals would pump a few inches of water from the river to the surrounding fields. This would freeze solid overnight, and for a modest fee one could skate all day.

Interspersed through the cold of that frozen term, I kept several appointments with the University Appointments Board, following "the system" in case it should throw up an interesting job but without any great inclination in any particular direction.

From this arose my one and only interview, happily on Exeat Day, March 15, at the end of term. After the morning train to London and lunch in a Joe Lyons, I presented myself at Unilever House by the Thames, where a recruiting board was examining potential recruits for their worldwide operation. I was received by a motherly secretary who offered me my expenses, and I was naïve enough to claim only 3/6d for my lunch. I was then ushered into a large boardroom and confronted by an array of businessmen, chaired, I gathered, by a Mr Van den Bergh, no less. He asked me one question: "What do you think of working in West Africa?"

"Not much."

He glanced round the other members of the board. "Doesn't look as though this one's an empire builder," and that was that.

Out of the building, up the embankment, a run across dear romantic Hungerford Bridge, a dash up the steps to Waterloo, and I just caught the 5 o'clock train home to Dorset and my last spring vacation. It was a bright, clear spring after the frosts, and there was still enough petrol to allow me to enjoy picnics on White Sheet Hill and at Worbarrow Bay.

At Worbarrow we climbed the Tout and lay on the top in the sunshine, watching a lone Sunderland flying boat patrolling up the Channel. It was the only reminder of war on an otherwise idyllically peaceful afternoon.

On April 9, 1940, the infamous day when Germany invaded Norway, suddenly the war became more imminent and menacing. By coincidence, that morning I received a letter from Norman Hughes, whose uncle was a group captain in the Air Ministry, and was, said Norman, interested in recruiting people like me "if the thing I had been working on was something called RDF". I wrote back to say it was, and please tell his uncle I was interested.

Of course these letters were monumental indiscretions, and Group Captain Lang, Deputy Director of Signals 4, made it very plain to Norman and me that we must NOT ever use these letters again, even if Norman did not know what they meant. Secrecy and security in wartime had to be absolute.

Apparently, my lapse was forgiven, and on the way back to Cambridge a week later for the final term I broke my journey in London for a brief interview, in a tiny Whitehall basement office, with Squadron Leader Orr-Ewing. He told me that if I did not intend to devote my whole life to radio, I would be wasting my time applying for a commission. For my part (profiting from my recent experiences with Unilever), I assured the squadron leader that I was absolutely devoted to radio, caught the next train to Cambridge and promptly posted my application to join the Royal Air Force.

On May 11 was the invasion of Belgium and Holland, as the Germans outflanked the Maginot Line. For me it brought a summons to London and an appearance before a selection board. Half-a-dozen officers of various ranks sat in a row behind a long table. I sat upright on a solitary chair in front of this imposing array, and I must have said the right things for I was promptly given a slip of paper and sent off to yet another Whitehall basement office to be medically examined.

Here I seemed to be about twentieth in a long queue, so imagine my pleasure when my name was called at once. "They must need me badly," I thought, "to call me before all those other chaps." I soon found out that I was not getting any special treatment when the Wing Commander MO did not even look at me. Instead he glanced at the paper placed in front of him by the orderly and waved me back to my place in the anteroom.

Half-an-hour later a junior doctor tested my reflexes and sent me back to wait. This was repeated several times with different examiners working on different parts of my anatomy, and then I was allowed to dress and go. I was learning to dress and go. I was learning that life in the RAF involved plenty of waiting about.

The end of May brought the Tripos final examinations (best forgotten) and then perhaps the only relaxing, truly undergraduate days of my whole three years in Cambridge. For the first time it was possible to enjoy life, and one whole day was spent paddling a canoe as far up river as possible, in company with Ken Hardaker—the first and last day on the river of my university career.

***

The first half of June was full of activity as the Germans struck deeper into France. Italy, sensing an easy victory for the Fascist powers, declared war on us, and we stood alone. It was a fine time to join up, I thought, as I busied myself with kitting out for war.

The faithful little Austin 7 gave us a gallant service, its back seat completely filled with the new trunk which I bought in Salisbury to take all my kit. This was completely zinc lined, iron bound and fitted with brass locks and hinges, and I had to pay no less than £2 for it. It was, in effect, my home for the next six years, over thousands of miles of ocean and very extreme climates. I have it still, strong and stout as ever; not bad service at under 5p a year!

While the remains of our expeditionary force struggled back from Dunkirk, Peggy and my mother sewed name tabs on all my clothing. The day Paris fell I completed my packing.

On June 16, while Churchill was proposing an act of union with France in a desperate bid to keep them fighting, the Germans broke through the already out-flanked Maginot Line. That was my last day as a civilian and we made one last, nostalgic trip to Worbarrow Bay.

Monday June 17 was perhaps the lowest-ever day as far as war with Germany was concerned; for me it was the day I donned the King's uniform—but not all at once. Oh no! A thrifty Air Ministry, in instructing me to report to an address in Leighton Buzzard, had sent a 3rd class rail warrant and instructions that I was not to put on uniform until after arrival, as officers had to travel 1st class. Thus it was still a flannel-trousered, sports-jacketed young man who said farewell to his nearest and dearest on Gillingham Station and once more was hauled off, by the power of steam, into a new life.

By the time I had crossed London to Euston and arrived from a stopping train to Leighton Buzzard, it was past lunchtime, and I did not stop to eat. I was setting off on foot, suitcase in hand, for the address on my instructions, when I overheard two people talking. "I never thought France would give in," said one, and that was how I learnt the news.

Later that day Winston Churchill, in his matchless rhetoric, told the nation that the Battle of France was over, and the Battle of Britain was about to begin, ending with the words: "Let us so bear ourselves, that if the British Empire lasts for a thousand years, men will say, 'This was their finest hour.'"

My own private thoughts, as I walked alone out of private life and into the service of King and country, were much more prosaic, something like, "Doesn't look too good, but it will be alright now I'm joining in." (Today that sounds frightfully conceited, but in reality, it expressed what most of us felt at that time. The possibility that we might lose the war just never entered our heads.)

The address I sought proved to be rather a large Victorian mansion, converted hurriedly into a Wing HQ. In a bathroom I put on my smart new uniform and wandered into the adjutant's office where I was immediately reprimanded:

43

"When you come into my office, you stand up straight and salute."

That was the sum total of my initial training, and the rest I had to pick up as I went along, for ten minutes later, still unfed, I was off on my first assignment. 80926, Acting Pilot Officer on Probation, RAFVR, B Samways, Administrative and Special Duties Branch, with a pay of eight shillings and six pence a day, was given a railway warrant to Holt (for West Beckham), sent off to the station in a van together with his trunk and suitcase, and caught the first train to London and off to war.

Now that I held the King's commission, I was entitled to travel 1st class, so feeling very important, I entered a compartment which already contained an elegantly dressed lady and gentleman. We were soon in conversation about the dramatic developments in France, and during a stop at Watford Junction he bought an evening paper to follow the latest news.

Glancing at his luggage, I realised that my companion was the conductor, Mr Sargent. Already well known, he was destined to be knighted for his services to music and to be world famous as Sir Malcolm Sargent in the postwar days of the televised promenade concerts.

Television! Although Britain had had the first television service in the world, this was closed down immediately on the outbreak of war, and the number of viewers then was so small that this curious decision passed without any public comment or official explanation. As I now knew, the short-wave lengths necessary for a television service were in the band now vital to RDF and no possibility of interference could be allowed. So Alexandra Palace was silenced for the duration.

I stayed overnight in the Great Eastern, peacefully enough despite an air raid warning, and caught an early train for Norfolk. In those days the rail network served the whole country, and it was possible to work out a route, by consulting Bradshaw or the ABC Guide, from anywhere to anywhere give or take a couple of miles.

But once off the main lines, interchanges and delays were numerous, so it took me nearly all day to get to Holt, the nearest rail point to West Beckham, where I was supposed to spend a week of temporary duty before going to the Radio School at Yatesbury on a formal posting. AMES West Beckham was the public title of this establishment, in conformity with the security needed to describe such places only as Air Ministry Experimental Station, and the general public, like indeed the rest of the Services, had no idea what went on there, behind the barbed wire.

Apart from a number of buildings, some protected with earth embankments, all that could be seen from outside were the two sets of aerial towers. Each of the four transmitter masts was a freestanding steel tower, 360 feet high, bearing outstretched arms on either side at the very top, and also at the 120 foot level. Between the upper and lower arms on each side were spiders' web-like arrays of wires and insulators, so that there were eight different wavelengths.

The receiver masts were also self-supporting towers, built entirely of wood and each 240 feet high, so that the receiving dipoles on their tops were at the same height as the centres of the transmitting aerial arrays. These were obviously very expensive constructions, and it was heartening to think that so much effort had been committed in peacetime. It was obvious that the RDF system I had joined was of the upmost importance in the air defence of Great Britain.

The first thing I did was to climb to the top of one of the transmitter towers, by way of the steel-rung ladders which zigzagged up from level to level. At the top, a narrow catwalk led out to each end of the extended arms, and if you stood at the end and jumped about, the whole structure would sway and spring under you, the most exhilarating feeling as you bobbed about in space.

I was fascinated by the aerial systems, perhaps because, as a physicist, I could understand their logic. By contrast, the workings of the transmitters and receivers (which seemed to come so easily to people who had been radio amateurs) were not to my liking, and I immediately took to studying the working of the system itself. The dimly lit operations room was the focus of my attention for the whole of the first night, for the air raid red alert started as darkness fell.

The cathode ray tube (CRT we called it) was essentially the same as today's black-and-white television tube: a beam of electrons, propelled by several thousand volts, shot up the tube and impinged on the phosphorescent screen to make a spot of light. Apply a voltage to a set of plates in the tube and you could make the spot move left or right. Apply another voltage to a set of plates at right angles and you could make the spot move up or down.

All you had to do now was to make the spot start its travel from left to right at the same time as you sent out your transmitter pulse, and then, if you got an echo from an aircraft, use that voltage to make the spot travel downwards. The distance travelled across the screen was a measure of the time taken for the pulse to go out and back at the speed of light.

Repeat this 25 or 50 times a second, and the screen showed you a steady, horizontal line of green light with a big U-shaped dip in it at the beginning (where the receiver was swamped by the direct signal from the transmitter) and a small V-shaped dip part way along. This V-shaped dip was the echo from your target aircraft, and the distance from the start of the U to the start of the V corresponded to the range of the aircraft. A direct scale of miles was applied to the tube, and this calibration could be checked by injecting an accurately calibrated signal, to give a little blip every 10 miles—the so-called "cali-pips". Already the RAF was generating a new jargon.

The direction of the returning signal was determined easily enough. It was collected on two sets of aerials, set at right angles and each one connected to its own coil, the two coils again being set at right angles to each other. Within each pair of coils was another, freely rotatable, coil which picked up the composite signal from the static coils, corresponding to the composite signal received from the two dipoles 240 feet up the mast.

As the operator twiddled his rotatable coil, he (or usually she, for WAAFs were increasingly being trained) could vary the signal strength from a maximum, when the coil pointed directly at the aircraft, to a zero, when it was pointing exactly 90 degrees away. The extinction point gave a much sharper reading than the maximum, and all the operator had to do, having read the range from the scale, was to swing the goniometer back and forth, through the extinction point, in ever-smaller arcs, until he sensed the exact setting corresponding to zero signal, which could be read off as a bearing on the calibrated gonio scale.

In theory it was dead easy. As I soon realised, in practice there was a lot more to do. The echo signals were very minute and had to compete with all the other random electromagnetic noise which was buzzing around, not only in the ether but also in the valves and circuits in the receiver. As you increased the amplification, this noise showed up as little echoes all across the trace so that the crisp, green, line became a dancing, shimmering set of points, not unlike a hayfield in appearance, and known, obviously, as "grass".

An average operator could detect a signal which was only about twice the strength of the noise (bear in mind that the signal and the noise were both intermittent; it was rather like lying on your face in a windy meadow trying to decide which blade of grass a hundred yards away was bobbing up and down just a bit more than the rest).

A good operator could do much better with skill and experience, by studying the base of the grass rather than the tips of the blades and could extract valuable information from the signal-to-noise ratio of only a weak echo. While the range could be determined to within a mile, the direction was not nearly so easy, and the first readings of angle could be 20 or 30 degrees out either way. A 20 degree error at 60 miles range is about 20 miles out in position, so an incoming track would often be plotted as a zigzag, narrowing down to a true course as the signal got stronger.

In a later chapter I will describe the system used to collate the information from the chain stations, but that night at West Beckham it was exciting enough to watch and study the operation of a single station. As the raid proceeded and hostile aircraft were plotted in across the North Sea, we could go out into the crisp night and try and get a "visual", or at least an "audible", on the enemy.

***

Before the end of the week I was posted to the Radio School, Yatesbury, and the amiable CO allowed me to leave on Friday afternoon—slow trains once more across East Anglia and on to London just too late for the Gillingham train, so I took the next best option and, late that night, reached Salisbury Station, still 24 miles from home. The only available local train went only to Wilton and at midnight I found myself setting out on foot with 20 miles still to go.

There was little enough traffic on the roads, especially at night, but anyone would stop for a serviceman in uniform, and a taxi driver gave me my first free lift for two miles until our ways diverged. For the next hour I plodded alone across the bleakness of the Salisbury Plain, and then a solo motorcyclist stopped. I climbed on the pillion and made good progress to Motcombe. From there I had only another two miles to walk, through the silent streets of Gillingham, down the town to the square, silently in with my own key, and silently to bed for a couple of hours' sleep before morning, when I descended from my attic room to my mother's surprise and delight.

I had to be at Yatesbury before 23.59 hours on Sunday (for some reason, the air force recognised only 23.59 and 00.01 hours, so presumably the war had to stop for two minutes every midnight). Now Yatesbury, I discovered, was in Wiltshire, and just 40 miles north of Gillingham, so I examined how I could best cover this distance, as often as possible, over the next few weeks.

It was not an easy train journey, with changes at Templecombe and Frome on the old Somerset & Dorset Joint Railway, but this had to suffice for my first trip. Even the train went only as far as Calne, and it was on foot that I approached the camp for my first glimpse of—well, it was to be my posting for the next two months and I had better make the most of it, but my heart sank at the sight. In the middle of miles of perfect, green, rolling hillside stood one mile square of nothing but dirty brown wooden huts, rows and rows of them, connected by concrete roads and concrete paths.

In the south eastern corner, just slightly remote from the rest, was a cluster of huts making the officers' mess. In the far northeastern corner, behind its own barbed wire security fence, stood the Radio School, so secret that the ordinary W/Ops training in the main camp were not allowed to know anything about it.

There were 23 of us on the course, ranging in age from 19 to 70 and from many different backgrounds, including a barrister and a banker. Everyone except me seemed to be an expert on radio theory and completely at home with valves and coils and chokes.

All I had to rely on was my basic physics knowledge and an ability to flannel my way out of trouble, so I copied out the circuit diagrams painstakingly, without properly understanding them, and invented my own shorthand for classifying valves as masculine, feminine or neuter, based on a fanciful connection between their current-passing functions and certain human physiological characteristics. Later in the war I was to find out that a pragmatic approach and immediate instinctive decision taking would serve me well, but for the present I just struggled to learn all the complicated circuits by rote.

I also gave a lot of thought to improving my personal lot in wartime and contingency plans for personal survival through the unknown future. The first priority was to get home as often and as much as possible, and I soon found that from 13.00 on Saturdays until 23.59 on Sundays I was free to leave camp, provided I was not on duty.

At 13.01 on the first Saturday I was off, not wasting time for lunch and accepting any lifts offered, although these usually lasted only a couple of miles. At Devizes one had to decide whether to follow the main road on an enormous detour through Salisbury or strike across country where traffic was minimal, so I followed the Salisbury Road with the hope of getting there in time for the last train. In the event I was much more fortunate: I came across a convoy of RAF lorries, three-tonners making up a complete mobile wireless station. The NCO said he was trying to get to Yeovil. I immediately offered to show the way across country and the way I chose just happened to go through The Square, Gillingham, so that I could alight at my front door.

Next afternoon it was back to Yatesbury by bicycle, 40 miles of cross-country, hilly roads, but in the few hours between I made Peggy learn by heart a code which I had devised. About the only education I had for war derived from prisoner of war escape stories I had read following the war of 1914–18, and I appreciated the value of being able to conceal a message in an otherwise innocuous letter.

Even a few words could convey a location or date, and apart from the possibility of being a prisoner of war it was nice to have a secret means of defeating the quite proper censorship which was imposed on all other ranks' mail, and randomly on occasional officers' letters.

To be useful, my code had to be not only unbreakable but also undetectable. Peggy was to share the secret with no one, except that if the situation ever arose that I was a prisoner in German hands, she could use her discretion in revealing a method to the Air Ministry.

In retrospect, all this seems a bit melodramatic. We did not then know what terrors might befall us, however, and I wanted to have something up my sleeve.

The first stage was to group the letters of the alphabet into a rough order of frequency, and then to pair off 13 such pairs of about equal frequency. These 13 pairs had to be memorised, for which I devised a sort of mnemonic beginning AS, EN, IT, OR, UP … and ending in VW, QZ.

A simple message was encoded by transposing each letter with its partner so that, for example, "WAR" became "VSO". The letters VSO were then to be demarcated by a simple yet elegant trick: the first part of a hand-written letter was to be ignored until a semicolon was reached, and then every letter up to the next and final semicolon was to be looked at closely. If the letter had a closed loop it was to be rejected, so that with slightly sloppy handwriting the meaningful letters could be marked. Our code group VSO could be conveyed as "I love you so".

As a final safeguard, and to avoid the need of over-elaborate care in writing, a looped letter could be changed to an unlooped letter, or vice versa, by placing an innocent dot next to it, thus: "I love you (dot on y) so".

As a final precaution against losing all contact if we were invaded and lost in the war, there was still America to fall back on, and so I decided on an advertisement in the *New York Herald Tribune* (the only American newspaper I could think of) as a means of making contact, in the new world, if we survived.

***

On my way back to Yatesbury I saw the wreck of a German bomber, a Heinkel, shot down into the Wiltshire fields and under an armed guard whose task it was to keep sightseers and souvenir hunters away while our intelligence officers extracted all the information possible. Using my uniform and identity papers, I passed the guard and examined the wreck at close quarters.

Suddenly the war seemed a lot closer, and I asked myself what I would have done if a German pilot had dropped out of the sky, armed with a pistol, for there were not enough small arms available at that date for issue to young acting pilot officers on probation. So, getting my hands on a gun of some sort became a priority in my personal survival plan, but several months were to pass before I found the way round the service procedure by the back door. My formal request for issue of a weapon, made to the adjutant of the Radio School, met with only a hollow laugh, and for the time being I stayed defenceless.

The Yatesbury course was eight weeks long, each week consisting of intense cramming of radio circuits from morning til night. How to be an officer and a gentleman was something we had to pick up as we went along, for we were needed on operations as soon as possible.

Yatesbury radar school   copyright believed expired

Each weekend (bar one when I had to stay miserably in camp as duty officer) I cycled down to Dorset and back, just for a few hours to be with Peggy, who would cycle to meet me on White Sheet Down, above Mere. It was a perfect summer of green fields, blue skies and larks singing their hearts out overhead: the picture of rural peace, but any day, we knew, might bring an aerial invasion to our blue skies and armed Germans to our green fields. Already the night skies were filled with the drone of many bombers overhead, and occasionally one heard a distant "thump" and knew that a bomb had landed only a few miles away.

These early days of August 1940 saw the start of the Battle of Britain in earnest, with daylight raids on the channel ports and attacks on channel shipping which virtually denied us the use of the English Channel. Clearly, the enemy began to appreciate why we always had fighters in the air to meet his attacks and on 12 August the main chain station at Ventnor on the Isle of Wight was attacked and put out of action.

On the very day of this attack we at Yatesbury sat full, formal examinations on all we were supposed to have learned, and on August 14 I was posted to MAPRE, Worth Matravers. A check with my friends showed that these initial postings were all near our homes, probably because the Air Ministry wished to economise on railway warrants rather than from any concern for our personal affairs.

This immediately disillusioned me from any idea that I was going to MAPRE as a scientist, and I should explain that the Ministry of Aircraft Production Research Establishment was only my old friend AMRE of Dundee, under a new name in a new location. (This move to a "safe" location away from the east coast was no sooner accomplished than France fell, and once more test flights out to sea were in danger of the enemy.)

The site, on St Albans Head near Swanage, housed not only the boffins in their wooden huts but also a fully operational CH station, and to this I was posted. I suppose I must have passed the examination, since I was transferred to the Technical Branch from the A&SD Branch and also dropped the "on probation" from my rank of acting pilot officer. All this I was to learn only a few days later, and first I had to proceed to RAF Warmwell by way of Rudloe Manor, an operations centre of Fighter Command, to complete my education on the RDF system of operations.

It seemed to me not unreasonable to turn this posting to advantage, so I consigned my trunk and bicycle to the railways goods services and accepted a ride in a friend's car to Rudloe where, after a cursory look at the Ops room and lunch in the mess, I took my leave inconspicuously, on foot, after signing the visitors' book to prove that I had actually been there.

The art of official travelling was to select a plausible rail route, with train times which appeared in Bradshaw, so that the journey took as long as possible, and preferably overnight, as the allowance is payable depended on the number of hours, with a sort of cash bonus if you could bridge the 23.59-00.01 hours bit, officially of course. The complicated local train journey from West Wiltshire to South Dorset was ideal for the time-wasting game, so off I went on my self-generated 24 hours of freedom, walking and hitchhiking as best I might, and heading for home.

By this time civilian petrol was decidedly short, and I walked as much as I rode, lugging a suitcase and carrying my gas mask and steel helmet, but I eventually got to Mere and then walked the four miles home. Next day, after a zigzag local train trip involving Templecombe and Blandford and Weymouth, I somehow got to Warmwell RAF station just as the air raid sirens started and was promptly bundled down into the trenches outside Station HQ.

When the panic was over I reported to the adjutant and conned him into giving me transport to work, on the grounds that my posting was urgent to this secret research establishment. I soon made out the familiar high steel towers of the transmitters, dominating the skyline above the rolling hills of Purbeck. Then, as we topped the rise of the intervening hill, I saw the squatter, stouter wooden towers of the receiving aerials, and below them, the operational buildings of the station, all set about with huts which housed the civilian research staff, including Ratcliffe and Lewis who had taught me at a Cambridge.

But I was in uniform and so I reported to my new CO, Flight Lieutenant Barham, who immediately made me responsible for the newly installed CHL, the low-flying cover station which was perched on the very edge of the cliff on St Albans Head itself and swept the seas across the French coast and the Channel Islands.

This was a toy after my own heart and, being at a much higher elevation than my first CHL at Anstruther, it was excellent for plotting shipping. To my surprise, there was no direct link to the navy, and I resolved to do something about this, as we shall see ... but first, I had to sleep somewhere, and for the first night I found a bed in a seaside boarding house at Swanage, too far off for my liking, and then I got myself billeted in the village.

The wartime powers available to the services were extensive, and all one had to do was to serve an order on a householder that henceforth "number rank and name" was billeted on him, giving him a ration card and the monetary allowance, and that was that. In practice, one usually sent an NCO in advance to "negotiate", that is to find out how many spare beds there were, to offer to come back accompanied by the civil police if necessary and preferably to settle the whole thing amicably and instantaneously. The nearest sizeable house to the station was the vicarage, and herein I promptly installed myself along with the admin officer, only walking distance from work.

Even this was not close enough, with most of the enemy activity at night, so I arranged a shake-down bed at my CHL so that I could be on hand at once for any excitement and then turned my thoughts back to the possibility of giving a helping hand to the navy. In the files I came across a reference to someone described as Flag Officer, Portland, and as I knew that the navy used flags for signalling, I thought this must be their equivalent to our RAF appointment of Signals Officer and just the chap I wanted.

Besides, it was a beautiful afternoon for a drive across the Dorset hills, so I authorised myself to use transport on form 247 and set off in the station van.

Portland naval base was protected by high walls and massive gates, for all the world like a mediaeval prison. A marine sentry inspected my identity card and referred me to the guardroom.

"I want to see the Flag Officer," I said, in all innocence.

"I am the duty Lieutenant, will that do?"

"Certainly not. I want to see the Flag Officer."

"What about?"

"That's secret".

There followed a couple of agitated telephone calls and then the bemused lieutenant, with a gesture of resignation as though to convey that he had done his best, ushered me across the courtyard and into the presence of—I knew at once, by the acres of gold braid all up his sleeves, contrasting so vividly with my own pathetic half ring—that this must be an Admiral no less. I saluted.

"Are you the Flag Officer, Sir?"

"I am. And who are you?"

I explained myself, and immediately aroused the admiral's interest. It may seem strange that there was not automatic liaison of this type I was proposing, but the fall of France had made everything different and Portland was suddenly very close to enemy bases. The admiral, it seemed, was much concerned that the enemy could mine his approaches from the air. Could I detect very low flying aircraft dropping mines?

It seemed probable that the course and speed of any such low-flying intruders would disclose their intention, and within half an hour we settled the whole thing, starting at once that very night, by the simple expedient of using the public telephone! We arranged a code word for shipping, and another for suspected minelaying aircraft: I was to telephone, give the code word, and then a range and bearing, without, of course, saying who or where I was, nor from what point the bearing was taken.

I am sure that the Air Ministry would have been horrified, for of course telephones were regarded as not secure, and anyway it was not my business to pass information direct to the Senior Service; but I was sublimely innocent in my belief that the right thing to do was to get on with the war and worry about the protocol later—if at all! This time I was lucky.

***

Every night now brought enemy activity, and the Crump! Crump! Crump! as sticks of bombs fell across the fields around us, and we did not know whether or not we were the target. I was given the task of plotting the bomb craters accurately on an ordnance map, to try to determine whether the lines of attack pointed to ourselves.

Now this was a wonderful job in the glorious summer mornings, and with a sergeant to drive the van I scoured the lanes all around the station and tramped miles over farms and downland, plotting the craters and collecting wicked-looking fragments of bomb casing to help identify what was being dropped on us.

One particular stick of bombs I shall always remember: the first crater was shallow, as though it were meant to fragment on impact, with splinters of steel scattered all around—just the job for the personnel and masts of an RDF station, I thought. This one had fallen in the field of rabbits at play, and a splinter had scythed off the top of a rabbit's head, to leave his body and lower jaw intact, with the crown of his head lying beside it and two surprised-looking ears still sticking upward from the furry scalp.

The sergeant and I followed the line of craters for half a mile, and I thought I had come to the end when I noticed a different hole, deeper and narrower, still in the same straight line. We peered and prodded at this hole for a while, until I came to the conclusion that if it had been a bomb, then it must have been a dud. Just in case, I advised the farmer to keep well away, and went home to lunch.

No sooner was I back at my desk after lunch than a white-faced sergeant came to me. "That bomb, Sir. It's just gone off."

Back we went to have a look, and sure enough, there was an enormous hole, just where we had been standing and prodding an hour before. It was a thoughtful young pilot officer who returned to the station to make an addendum to his report.

That night, during yet another air raid, the main station receiver aerial system developed a fault, so I took a mechanic, a torch and a pair of pliers, and climbed the mast to investigate. On the way up the 240 foot of laddering, I tried to figure out whether I was safer up in the air or down on the ground if any of the bombs came too close, and took some comfort from the fact that, according to official doctrine, the mast I was climbing was supposed to stay upright with two of its four legs shot away.

The biggest danger seemed to lie in our own forces, for around the station were a number of anti-aircraft posts, with Bofors guns and machine guns trained skywards, and their crews, of course, at action stations. So we climbed in the dark, and when we had to use the torch to locate and fix the fault, we did our best to keep cupped hands under the light.

**

Sunday August 25 was yet another perfect summer's day, and Flight Lieutenant Barham decided that it was safe to leave me in charge while he had an afternoon on the beach, after many days and nights of continuous duty. Thus I spent the day in the receiver room of the main CH station, leaving my own CHL to look after itself.

Plots now began to appear over the Channel Islands, and although these got menacingly bigger, they hardly moved. It was clear that a mass attack was assembling, using the islands as a rallying point, and with Ventnor CH out of action, it seemed highly probable that we were the target. After all, apart from our operational station, we had, on the same site, the whole research organisation, with, presumably, the best scientific brains in the country.

The trace on the cathode ray tube was an awesome sight. Instead of the normal tiny V shaped depression, which would denote an aircraft at that range, a great jagged valley appeared, dipping down to the bottom of the screen and covering some 10 miles of the time base. Now, estimating the number of aircraft from such an echo was much more an art than a science, but putting all the factors together, I gave my personal authority to the operator to increase his estimate to 50-plus. This was going to be a mass raid, and the first on our part of the coast.

Did the enemy think that, with Ventnor out of action, he was turning the flank on our RDF system? Surely, he must have monitored our transmissions and knew just where we were. Perhaps over-impressed with the idea of our own importance, I became more and more convinced that we were in for it.

We had just had a new toy installed for the benefit of the boffins. This was a cine camera, focused on the cathode ray tube, and I had been asked to take a film if any really good echoes appeared. This seemed just the opportunity, so I switched the thing on and made the first film of the RDF system in actual warfare operation.

(I never saw this film rerun, and it was not until later that I learned what happened to it. This was the very week when Mr Winston Churchill made his historic speech including the immortal words "never in the field of human conflict was so much owed by so many to so few", but what the public did not know was that he had just sent Sir Henry Tizard to America to disclose to our potential allies our latest scientific discoveries, including all that we then knew about RDF. "My" film of the raid of 25 August was flown out to America that same night, on Churchill's personal orders, to help convince the Americans that we were not beaten.)

None of this I knew at the time, and I quite forgot the cine camera as I watched the menacing echo begin to close in, and grow even bigger, as the aerial armada set out directly towards us. It was difficult to escape the passing thought that, possibly—even probably—we should all be dead in half an hour. I do not recall, on that occasion at least, feeling frightened, and I soon went outside to try for a visual and to check on the count. It was a perfect summer's afternoon, with clear blue skies and somewhere a lark singing, the only noise in the heavens.

Then my secret knowledge of what was coming over the horizon was broken to the public by the strident wailing of the air raid warning, rising and falling in pitch and volume for two minutes, followed by profound silence. Then, barely perceptible at first, a persistent hum which seemed to come from all over the sky, directionless. I ran in to report an audible, then out again to try to catch the first glimpse of the enemy. They came, little specks of light glinting from Perspex canopies, in massive formation, for all the world like a peacetime fly-past. I counted roughly up to 50 at one time, as they overflew the station and passed inland. It was not our turn, today at least.

I was clearly not the only one to be impressed by the sight of a mass formation of bombers which could have scatter-bombed our whole research station into oblivion. Despite our early warning, our own fighters could hardly disturb the massed bombers, so great was the strength of the escorting Messerschmitt 109s. Indeed, it seemed that the object of the mass bomber raids was to draw out our last reserves of fighters, hopefully to be shot down as a prelude to the invasion.

Another factor in those desperate days was the need to keep our fighter section either over land or close inshore, so that the chances of saving the pilots alive to fight again was balanced in our favour. Locally, all this added up to the immediate realisation that MAPRE, perched on St Alban's Head, was extremely vulnerable, and so it happened that next day, returning to the vicarage for lunch, I found the vicar's wife in a state of great alarm. Two strange men in civilian clothes had just walked in, given no names or identity, and told her that she would probably be evacuated "so that her house could be taken over".

(It must be remembered that at this time both the British and the German high commands regarded an invasion as a matter of when, not if. All church bells were silenced and their ringing would mean that the invasion had started. Fresh in all our minds was the ease with which Norway had been occupied, aided by the treachery of Quisling and the so-called fifth column. It was an offence under wartime regulations to "spread despondency and alarm".)

How was I to know that one of the two mysterious strangers who had so alarmed my landlady was none other than that very distinguished civil servant, A.P. Rowe, who was in charge of the whole research establishment and who had, that morning, visited a number of large houses in the area with a view to dispersing his scientists away from our so-obvious target for an air raid?

Perhaps, I thought, the invasion was imminent, and our British Quislings were hoping to throw the civilian population into confusion and turmoil. So I just picked up the telephone and informed the police at Swanage.

As I approached the gatehouse after lunch I was met by my CO, Flight Lieutenant Barham, in something of a panic. He, poor innocent, had just been savaged by Rowe for "unwarrantable interference by the RAF into the affairs of MAPRE" and he thought that I ought to account for my actions. It seemed that I had not only ruined the great man's plans, but also the secrecy in which he was trying to carry them out. Unpleasant words like "court martial" were being used. What had I to say for myself?

By now I was beginning to pick up some of the basic rules of self-defence in service life, so I retired to the orderly room, commandeered a typewriter from the clerk, and addressed a memorandum marked SECRET, to my CO.

I began with the proper: "Sir, I have the honour to report …" then gave a brief account of the events and ended up: "I will be pleased to give you or to the Superintendent of MAPRE any other information in my possession.

"I have the honour to be, Sir, etc" and signed it, not forgetting to add the P/O, RAFVR after my name.

That was the last I heard of it, and we all went back to the task of fighting the Germans instead of one another.

For the next two weeks, the Battle of Britain raged fiercely by day and by night, with the balance shifting towards night time raids on London. Official figures on aircraft lost and enemy planes shot down were at best speculative and at worst straightforward propaganda. Behind the facade of "official figures" the truth began to emerge that German losses were greater than British, and that Göring might not, after all, be able to sweep the RAF from the skies and clear the way for an invasion during the summer months of 1940.

It was indeed fortunate that he underestimated the importance of our RDF system, for we were extremely vulnerable as well as being indispensable. Had Göring concentrated his attacks entirely on the CH and CHL stations for only one day, he could have largely obliterated our effective fighter opposition, for Hurricanes and Spitfires were useless unless given the time to climb to operational height. Our stations were soft targets, protected at best by a few machine guns and light AA.

The pre-war CH stations were just huts, on clifftops, with a few pathetic sandbags, perhaps. My own CHL, being important as the local test bed for the research station, enjoyed the luxury of one Lewis gun and a handful of soldiers to guard us against air attack. To the south and below us, cliff paths led down to the sea with nothing, not even a strand of barbed wire, between us and the enemy. In fact, after a night in the operations room I would go down at dawn to bathe in the sea.

On Friday 13 September came a signal from Air Ministry: "80926 Pilot Officer B Samways posted to AMES Skendleby to Command. To report to RAF Manby forthwith." Manby, I found, was in Lincolnshire, so this was another journey to turn to advantage: in an hour my luggage and I were threading our ways through the intricacies of the Somerset and Dorset railway system to arrive at Gillingham station by early evening, once more to the surprise and delight of my sweetheart.

These brief, snatched reunions were very precious, especially as this time I was off to the east coast, and from rural Dorset that was almost to the ends of the Earth. Who could say when we should next meet, or where?

Chapter 5

AMES Skendleby

The 9.07 train next morning hauled me off to Salisbury and London. I hung out the window and waved to the forlorn little figure on the platform until a cloud of smoke and steam, reflected down as we chattered under the road bridge, obliterated the last glimpse, and then I settled down to begin a new adventure. London had suffered much from the bombing, and my train could not reach Waterloo. Instead, everyone had to get out at an obscure station in the suburbs, and here I found help from the RTO. (Every station of any size had its rail transit officer. These were splendid fellows, almost without exception elderly Guards' officers, and they were most helpful.)

The RTO assigned me to the back of an army lorry, together with a number of other servicemen of diverse ranks and units, and this probed its way through the back streets towards central London, turning back from time to time as we met barriers and diversions because of rubble blocked streets, unexploded bombs or burning houses.

Eventually, I was routed onto a train for the northeast, and it was evening before I reported to RAF Manby, in company with a young navigator who, two nights before, had been dropping bombs on Berlin. Manby was a prewar station, with a peacetime officers' mess, so after reporting to the SDO I was able to get a bed for the night and my first food since breakfast.

Next morning, armed proudly with my signal posting me to Skendleby to command, I persuaded the adjutant to give me road transport for the 20-mile journey to my new assignment.

AMES Skendleby was the first CHL station to be sited a few miles back from the coast. The loss of those few miles in range was quite unimportant compared with the advantage of height above sea level, for the land slopes away gently eastward all the way to the North Sea, and my unimpeded narrow beam could sweep the optical horizon over a much greater area than the preceding CHL at Ingoldmells, on the sand dunes by the shore.

Ingoldmells was reduced to a care and maintenance status and was also under my command, as I learned from Flight Lieutenant Geoffrey Tookey, whom I was replacing. Tookey gave me the briefest introduction to my new domain: in the middle of a large field was the familiar gantry, topped by the usual rotating aerial array and straddling the operations hut. Some attempt was being made to build a blast wall round the hut, out of railway sleepers and earth. At the gate stood a guard hut, for we had a platoon of elderly reservists as guards, and along the western boundary were two other huts, one being my office and stores while the other housed the guard, the only personnel living on site. All the RAF were in billets.

Tookey was anxious to be off, so I signed a slip of paper for him without more ado, accepting total responsibility that my new command had been handed over in good order (after the war Tookey was to become an eminent QC), and then, less formally, took over his bed and board in Claxby Manor farm, a short walk down a narrow lane towards the sea.

I was very proud of my new command and more than a little awed at the thought of my total responsibility for some 30 airmen and for defending my part of the east coast when the invasion came. No-one had given me any basic training in service life or in any aspects of command or man-management. At 21 I was younger than all the men I commanded, and at three months my length of service was shorter than that of any airman.

But the need to fling resources into the air defence of the country meant that such risks just had to be taken, and the only criterion was to keep the station on the air. I never ceased to be grateful for the extreme tolerance shown to us amateurs as we muddled our way through, or around, the correct RAF procedures, provided only that we kept the station working.

On all operational matters we were responsible to 60 Group HQ, and we had the facility, if necessary, to contact them direct through our own RDF telephone network, with lines continuously open to Fighter Command at Stanmore, but all this was secret from the rest of the RAF. Nominally, we reported to RAF Manby for pay and discipline, but that was all. (And one day the group captain commanding my parent station turned up at the gate, to see just what was this AMES in his charge at Skendleby. I refused to admit him, as I was quite entitled to do.)

I was indeed fortunate in having as my orderly room corporal a Corporal Alger, a Yorkshireman who had been in the ill-fated expeditionary force to France in 1939. He rapidly taught me what I had to do as a commanding officer and looked after the whole administration for me, leaving me free to concentrate on operations. I spent many hours, especially at night, taking watch myself to gain experience as an operator and studying the possibilities for estimating the numbers of aircraft in a formation from the behaviour of the echo.

There were of course long hours when nothing happened, and it was fatally easy for an operator to lose concentration after an hour spent staring at the wobbly green line, trying to detect the first moment when one wobble seemed to be a bit bigger than all the others, but there was keen rivalry to be the first station to pick up a new track. I was acutely aware of the danger of a very low-flying sneak attack which would not be seen at all by the powerful CH stations and might be visible only to our beam for 10 or 15 miles.

Most people in Britain in 1940 had an unshakeable faith that we were safe in our island home, come what may. Our navy was the best in the world, and England was full of soldiers back from Dunkirk. One had a mental image of rows of soldiers standing shoulder to shoulder on the beaches, ready and willing to stick bayonets into any Huns who tried to land.

I was as bad as the rest, until one day when I took a trip out to the seashore to see my unit at Ingoldmells. All the way to the sea, and all along the sands when I got there, not a soldier was to be seen. Some barbed wire, to be sure, but no guns, no lorries, no ships, nothing! That night, taking a turn at operating, sweeping my beam across the horizon from coast to coast, I had the same complacent feeling that everything was alright because "somebody out there would be on watch".

Somebody? Wake up, chum, it's not "somebody"; it's you! Knowing as I did that there were no fixed defences between me and the North Sea, one's instinct for self-preservation took over, and I used every means I could think of to ensure that my crew gave the earliest warning: promises of reward, threat, surprise inspections, anything to keep them on the alert.

One night I came back to the station on foot after dark and found no sentry at the gate; he was safely in his hut with the door shut. So I quietly climbed over the high barbed wire gate, tiptoed to the platoon hut, woke up the platoon sergeant and ordered him to put his sentry on a charge. The poor man had no defence and I felt quite sorry for him secretly, but I had to show that orders were to be obeyed.

I was much disturbed that we had no means of defence except six rifles which looked as though they had been in store since the Boer War—and probably had been. Should we be invaded, I had an absolute duty to see that our secret documents were dropped in the lead-lined box of sulphuric acid kept for the purpose, and to see that "the split" was blown up.

The split was the very latest secret fitted to our receiver aerial. It was effectively an electric motor, spinning a rotary coupling which caused a beam to wobble alternately about 1 degree left and 1 degree right of its true direction. It therefore received two echoes, displayed side-by-side on the time base, and it was possible to set the aerial direction very accurately by just moving it until the two echoes were the same size. It was rather like having two spotlights on a stage and marking precisely the point where the two circles overlapped.

Anyway, this was so secret that it was fitted with a couple of pounds of TNT permanently installed, fused and wired, just above the operator's head, so that it could be blown to pieces at a moment's notice by connecting the wires to a battery.

It seemed to me that it was desirable to be able to keep the enemy out, for a few minutes at least while I saw to these niceties. But all I had was a barbed wire fence which I had just climbed over under a sentry's nose and which was anyway far too big a perimeter to be defended with six rifles.

So I went off to Manby and sought help from the armaments officer, who kindly offered to come down and look over my problem. I conveniently overlooked the fact that, like his group captain, he had no pass to enter our AMES, and I welcomed him in. At first, he said there was nothing he could do for me and the best thing was to concentrate my six rifles to defend the central operations block, opening fire only when the enemy started to breach the wire fence. It was useless to dig trenches at our perimeter and hold that. As for more weapons, there were none available.

But happily, his eyes lit upon the bomb rack, a trophy salvaged from a crushed German bomber and lovingly restored to working order by some of the station mechanics. It was their great pride and joy, and they demonstrated to my guest the working of the electro-mechanical release.

"I must have that," he said, going on to explain that he had to train armourers in dealing with crashed enemy bombers, perhaps still containing their bomb loads, and he badly needed just such a rack for training purposes. Here was an opportunity to be exploited, and after a quick round of bargaining we made a trade: he would give me two .300 calibre US machine guns, 1000 rounds of ammunition and, for my personal use, a .455 Colt automatic, while I would hand over one Luftwaffe bomb rack in working order.

Next morning, I loaded the rack into our 30 cwt van—the only transport I had—and drove off to Manby where we effected the swap, and I bore my trophies back to Skendleby. There on the wall was a big notice: "Where is our bomb rack?"

I was aghast, not so much at the insubordination and affront to my authority as to think that I had such a bunch of petty-minded schoolchildren with which to try to defend my station and myself against real Germans armed with real bombs and bullets.

It was time my men and I got to know each other better, so I ordered my faithful corporal to parade all hands, minus only the watchkeeper, at the 2 pm changeover. When he reported to me in my office that "parade was present and correct, Sir" I put on my cap and gloves, waited five minutes and marched out to take the first of the only two parades I was to hold in the whole of my service.

Then I made a little speech, in roughly the following terms: "Some ignorant and stupid moron among you has seen fit to put up a notice about the bomb rack. I gave it to the armaments officer at Manby because he needs it, which you don't. Moreover, he is helping to give us some machine guns which might just help to save your stupid lives, if we get attacked.

"Now you know. And if I ever again get any insubordination like this, I'll find out who did it and have his guts for garters. Corporal, dismiss the parade."

That seemed to do the trick, and I had no further trouble of any sort. Relationships between ranks in the RAF were easy-going, with little of the formal discipline affected by other services. This was especially so in the RDF business since we were nearly all volunteers, and the few senior regulars in the game just had to take us as we were.

We quickly dug a couple of gun pits to take the two tripod mountings, but when we had unboxed and degreased the guns, we found that there were no mounting swivels to connect the guns to tripods. Ludicrous as it now seems, I actually paid tuppence out of my own pocket to buy an old bicycle frame from a local cycle shop. This we attacked with a hacksaw and a file to produce hand-made adaptors to bridge the trans-Atlantic gap between the British tripods and the American machine guns. What a way to go to war!

***

I extracted one more favour from my friend the armaments officer. As I was anxious to know what would happen if I ever had to blow the demolition charge, he offered to explode a similar charge as a demonstration. This we arranged in a remote corner of the site, using a couple of concrete blocks instead of the secret split device as a target. We stood a couple of hundred yards away, like children at a fireworks party, and connected the two wires to the poles of a battery.

The result was shattering, in every sense. Bits of rubble whistled past our ears and plopped onto the hut roofs. No trace of the concrete blocks remained, and the stunning detonation was followed by reverberating echoes from surrounding woodlands and by the squawking of pheasants for miles around.

The locals thought it was a German attack on us ("Those poor boys up at the station," said one good lady), and the police telephoned to ask why there had not been an air raid warning? It seems the bang was heard over a three-mile radius, and all this from a miserable two-pound charge.

I did not really mind the interest from the locals, and in fact encouraged any false rumour as a cover for our secrecy. I did not attempt to deny (or confirm) that we were engaged in developing explosives, and refused to confirm the other popular story, that we were drilling for oil.

My main contact for keeping in touch with public opinion was Raymond Chatterton, the farmer's son. Raymond had his own theory that we were receiving radio signals and redirecting them to aeroplanes, and to this I listened politely, without comment, as we shared family meals in the farmhouse kitchen.

This was real, old-fashioned farmhouse living, with home-made butter churned by hand in a wooden vat, and home-cured bacon from a home-killed pig; and for weeks after a pig killing there were home-made sausages and home-made brawn. Apple tart and cheese were served as a first course, in the Lincolnshire fashion, to be followed by the meat course. A never-failing spring ran constantly from the foot of a crag across the lane, producing a little rill that flowed through the farm, powering a hydraulic ram which plop-plopped incessantly, day and night, to squirt the fresh spring water a few drops at a time into the header tank in the farmhouse roof. I slept in a deep, deep feather bed, no doubt home-made from generations of home-plucked poultry.

Life in the farmhouse seemed unchanged and unchanging from centuries past, in strong contrast to the war being fought overhead and the technological marvel of the RDF system. It was as though I switched centuries every time I walked up the lane from Claxby and entered my barbed wire compound and my secret world of ultra-short-wave radio and hostile aircraft echoes.

As September mellowed into October, the daylight raids dwindled, and the main Luftwaffe effort went into night bombings of our major ports and cities, while our own bombing effort, night after night, gave us much plotting, to and fro, across the North Sea. Most evenings we saw formations of Whitley and Hampden bombers heading east and climbing laboriously into the gloom as they headed out

70

over the coast. We dutifully reported all visuals and then followed the plots, trying to improve our estimation of numbers by relating the behaviour of the echoes to the size of the formations we had seen overhead.

Towards dawn we plotted the stragglers home, paying particular attention to any flying too low for the CH coverage: our last plot on a ditching friendly could be vital to the life and death of the crew. Even when an echo had faded from our trace, we could still sometimes continue to plot the IFF response, for this system, fitted to British aircraft, received and re-transmitted, amplified, our pulses of radiation. It did this intermittently, so that every few seconds an echo from an aircraft showing IFF (Identification Friend or Foe) would suddenly grow bigger for half a second and then drop back to normal, and these last flickers from a dying aircraft could still give us a range and bearing when the RDF signal was too weak to discern.

Good flying nights for us were good, also, for the enemy, and we frequently plotted each-way traffic at both ends of the night. One enemy victim we assisted in intercepting was a Heinkel He 111 which crashed on the beach at Chapel St Leonard's on October 3 between the tide lines. I was soon on the spot and crawled over the carcass with an officer from the technical branch who was looking for secret devices or anything unusual. The DF (directional finding) system was standard and of no interest, so I helped myself to the rotating loop aerial as a souvenir and also to a most useful empty parachute bag. The latter gave me service as a kit holdall through the war and for years afterwards, while the former, which had no useful function, I converted into a jewellery casket with a curved hinged lid. It stands on my wife's dressing table today.

Heinkel rotating loop aerial   Jewellery box

I also tried to recover one of the bent propeller blades as a souvenir for the station in place of their bomb rack, but all efforts to remove this were defeated by the strength of German engineering and the rising tide.

In retrospect, of course, it was extremely foolish of me even to approach a wrecked enemy aircraft, with no real need to do so, for unexploded bombs and even deliberate booby-trapping were an obvious danger. (One of those who was on my Yatesbury course was blown up later in the war, doing just the same thing.) At the time I just never thought about it, for this was the first time I had ever had a chance even to see the inside of any aeroplane, let alone an enemy warplane.

As the rising tide reached the wreck and we were retreating up the beach to our truck, a lone, leisurely aircraft flew slowly out of the mist to the north, apparently searching the coastline from a height of only a few hundred feet. It was a Junkers Ju 88. We didn't wait for it to turn and come back, having no wish to be shot up or bombed.

***

All my troops were billeted at random in isolated farm cottages, which was most inconvenient for transport at shift change times, so I re-billeted them in Willoughby, a village to the east, where there was a railway station, a church and a pub. I also moved my own billet to a house called Heliopolis, where I was well looked after by Mrs Riddington, a motherly soul who introduced me to the life of the village, such as it was: a social in the village school room on Saturday evenings and the nonconformist chapel in Alford on Sunday nights.

These were only brief interludes from duty, for I worked a seven-day week and was on call via the telephone whenever I was away from the station. This was not so much the overzealousness of youth (although I did take pretty seriously my responsibility for fighting my little bit of the war) as the fact that one had little interest in a private life separated from England, home and beauty. The whole idea was to get the war over and then pick up the strings where they were dropped in 1939.

However, even the war had to wait if there was the possibility of a game of rugby, and a chance meeting with a Captain Green of the Sherwood Foresters led to a local challenge: in two days we organised a pitch and goal posts, and duly on November 13 we defended the honour of the RAF by beating the army by a narrow margin. I had the good luck to score the winning try, which did my authority more good with the troops than any badges of rank.

Next day, November 14, it was back to the war with a vengeance, for this was a day, or rather a night, to go down in history, although I did not then know it as I set off southwards at teatime in a little blue-grey RAF van driven by a civilian boffin from Wing HQ. This lad had mentioned casually that he was "driving down to Stanmore" and I promptly begged a lift, for this was something I just had to see. My excuse for deserting my station (which I made only to myself, thinking it better not to ask) was that it would help the efficient operation of my station if I could see what was at the other end of our telephone link and find out what they did with all the plots we sent down to it.

It was a crisp, cold but very clear night, the full moon rising as we sped down the A1 and into Hertfordshire. "A real bombers moon tonight," we said as I guided the driver through Hatfield to Watford, past my old house and the place of my birth and on to the legendary Bentley Priory at Stanmore.

This was not only the headquarters of Fighter Command, under the awesome command of "Stuffy" Dowding, but, deep underground, were housed the filter room and operations room where all our RDF plots were collected and from where the fighter defence of the country was directed.

But how to get in? My driver had a legitimate business at the HQ, and our service passes gained us entry easily enough at the main gate, but all my friend could do was to show me the entrance to "the drain" (as it was popularly called) and leave me to try my luck. The armed sentry inspected my 60 Group pass, which was apparently of a secure enough rating, but what was my authority to enter the holy of holies? I was OC RAF Skendleby, I said, and had been assigned for temporary duty at the Filter Room.

It did not seem necessary to state that I had done my own assigning, and I was allowed in.

A long sloping tunnel led down to the filter room, so called because the scattered information from the various chain and CHL stations was "filtered" or refined to give the best composite picture of aerial traffic. This system, I learned, gave us a unique advantage over the enemy and I studied it closely.

Around a large tabletop map of the east and south coasts sat a number of WAAF operators, each wearing a head-and-breast telephone set connected directly to the chain station and placing counters directly onto the grid reference of each plot received. Once several plots were in position, usually from more than one station, a junior officer would assess the most likely position and direction of the aircraft and place an arrow to mark this.

The filter officer bore in mind the quality of the information laid before him, particularly that the range indicated was likely to be more accurate than the direction, and he could often therefore assess the position of an aircraft accurately from range alone if more than one station could "see" the aircraft, however faintly. To assist in this, concentric circles were painted around each CH station.

74

Thus a track of advancing arrows was soon established, and beside each track was put a little display showing the controlling filter officer's assessment (Friendly, Hostile, or X), and his guesses as to the height and number of aircraft.

Each track was given a serial number, and (here was the beauty of the system) only the filtered information was read out and replotted in the Ops Room, where the controller could give his undivided attention to the tracks of hostiles and friendlies alike and could despatch or recall fighter squadrons as the battle developed. He surveyed the whole scene from a raised balcony, while on the wall opposite were state boards for each squadron and station, showing the up-to-the-minute position—airborne, landed, refuelling, rearming or other information.

Beside the controller sat liaison officers from the navy and the AA command and behind him, from time to time, appeared some very senior officers indeed. At the sight of so many broad blue rings and gold braid, I prudently shrank back into the shadows—but not quickly enough, for a peremptory enquiry came down from the top deck to know who I was and what I was doing there. The ADC who brought the message advised me to keep out of sight and say that I was working for ORS.

"What is ORS?"

"You know, Operational Research Section, the boffins who study the system."

"OK, thanks for the tip, I'll keep my head down."

The controller probably had so much to worry about that he forgot all about me, and the ADC did not have to lie on my behalf. I kept to the back of the filter room and followed the course of the air war on the filter plot, which of course had all the friendlies and hostiles displayed even earlier than in the Ops room.

***

It soon became clear that tonight was something special, with near maximum effort from both sides. Outgoing tracks of the streams of our bombers crossing the North Sea were crisscrossed by incoming hostiles, but this time the incoming tracks were not converging on London, for an all-out effort was being made to smash the city of Coventry in the heart of the manufacturing Midlands.

The destruction of Coventry Cathedral, probably unintended, was a propaganda gift to the British and gave rise to some memorable press photographs. This night, the "we can take it" spirit of London was generated again in the provinces, and almost certainly the rise in our morale outweighed any military advantage to the enemy. But this assessment was to come much later.

We all felt an unusual air of excitement as the plotting table filled with more and more tracks, and the balcony filled with more and more senior officers. There was a curiously unreal atmosphere, a sort of detachment even, as though we were playing some giant game of Monopoly in a well-lit, warm, secure, underground environment. The WAAF plotters moved the pieces across the table in an apparently unconcerned, professional manner, with all the indifference of a croupier as to who won or lost.

Yet I kept reminding myself that those little plastic arrows were, at this very moment, matched by real bombers, crewed by real flesh and blood airmen, many of whom would be dead before dawn. Those Red-Alert warnings displayed over most of England were matched by whistling bombs and blazing buildings as Coventry suffered the main weight of the attack. I was selfishly grateful that tonight, at least, Dorset was safe.

As the night wore on, the two-way traffic continued, but now the incoming tracks were mostly our own returning Bomber Command aeroplanes. Mostly, that is, because the Germans were apt to fly in occasional intruders to mingle with our returning bombers and shoot them down on their approaches to their home runways. For this reason, the accurate identification of incoming tracks was vital, and although all our aircraft were fitted with IFF which should, in theory, mean that the echoes from them would be

76

identified as friendly, there was always the chance that the equipment was faulty—or the more sinister possibility that the enemy was using captured equipment to fly under false colours.

The main streams of returning RAF bombers, flying at normal height to their home stations, were arriving roughly to a predictable timescale; but what of the lame ducks? I could picture anxious station commanders counting in their returning flocks as they played, in real life, the board game we were following in our secure underground setting.

Inevitably, as dawn approached, my attention became fixed on a couple of loan tracks, still far out over the North Sea, which Skendleby alone was tracking although their IFF signals were still just visible to other low-flying stations. They were therefore down near sea level, flying so desperately slowly, struggling to make a landfall, perhaps flying on one engine, perhaps on fire; and here we were, watching them die. One after the other, the last plots from Skendleby were reported, and I knew that they must be skimming the wave tops if they were below even our low-flying cover.

Still, for a few minutes weakening IFF signals showed until these too suddenly stopped, and I knew they had been ditched. The feeling of helplessness was overpowering, and I could not stop myself from leaning forward and whispering to the WAAF plotter on the Skendleby line, "Can't we do something?"

She looked at me, coldly, professionally, and said, "Air-sea-rescue will have been given the plot, Sir." But as she turned back to the table I caught the glint of a tear in her eye.

I never knew what had occupied my two boffin companions at Bentley Priory all that night, so much later, when I learned of the "headache and aspirin war" I wondered if they had been forewarned of the Coventry attack and were at HQ to study the result of their Wing HQ radio countermeasures.

At any event, their interest in Stanmore ended at dawn and so, sleepless, supper less and breakfast less we drove off again to Lincolnshire to resume our own personal little wars, while the people of Coventry fought the fires among the rubble and anxious station commanders still kept their dawn vigil, hoping against all probability that their missing aircraft had somehow, somewhere, managed to reach home.

A retrospective note tells me that on that same day, November 14, I had been promoted to acting flight lieutenant, the rank appropriate to my post of station commander of an AMES—but I never knew this until weeks later, and for the rest of my stay at Skendleby I still wore my pathetic, thin, pilot officer's rings. But my days there were already numbered.

On my desk next morning lay a signal instructing me to select six airmen for posting overseas. All of a sudden, it seemed, the awesome responsibility of being able to play at being God had been thrust upon me, for I now had to alter the lives of six men in a profound but unpredictable manner. To go overseas was, pre-war, almost equivalent to stepping off the edge of the world; and certainly, in my pre-war way of thinking, anyone who went to America or Australia just never came back.

So on what basis was I to decide which of my men would (it seemed to me) live or die? Should I call for volunteers? Or select the least useful? Or seek the advice of Corporal Alger?

In the end, I looked up the records and then named, as far as possible, the unmarried and the youngest, and then I turned my mind to other things. The need for total secrecy over our work was impressed on us all and was remarkably well maintained. Perhaps there was some element of self-preservation in this, but we all knew how defenceless we were to air attack—if the enemy only knew where to find us and what we were doing.

As part of our security I instituted passwords, changed daily, to be given by incoming shift personnel to the sentry. It was not so much the extra security this provided, but the use of such a rigmarole helped to keep all hands alive to the dangers.

I also wrote out a list of code words, known only to me, which the duty NCO could use over the public telephone to pass me information at night. These were words for things such as: "Station off the air", "Warning of possible gas attack" etc, and I remember vividly the last two phrases on the list: "You have been posted" (LETTER BOX) and "You have been posted overseas" (HOLY SMOKE).

Chapter 6

"Holy smoke"

On the evening of November 2 the phone rang in my billet. "There's a signal just in, Sir. HOLY SMOKE, Sir".

"Thank you, Corporal. Send the truck and I'll come in."

I soon had the signal pad in my hand and read, "80926 P/O B Samways to be inoculated and kitted to Middle East standards and hold himself in readiness for posting overseas." This was the big adventure, and it was happening to me. Of course I had no idea where I was really going, for even early in the war I had understood that troop movements were sometimes concealed by the publication of false information. For all I knew I might be going to Iceland or Australia.

One thing was certain: I was going somewhere, but when? I had, it seemed, only just arrived at Skendleby, for I had been just nine weeks in my command when the orders came, and that was the longest time I had stayed in one place since joining up.

Next morning, I reported to the MO at Manby and got my armful of injections and drew what kit I could from the stores. Soon came a more definitive signal from 60 Group: I was to spend a week at Yatesbury, have a week's leave and go to Uxbridge on 15 December. The sooner the better, I thought, and caught the next train from Willoughby Station to Kings Cross, where I stayed the night in the Great Eastern before taking the early-morning train from Paddington down the old GWR network and branch lines to get to Yatesbury.

Nobody knew much about me there, but it seemed that I was expected to brush up my knowledge of mobile units, then comprising a type 2 transmitter, the TR 2, and the mobile receiver RM1A. The theory of these beasts I had covered in my course, and there were no new developments, as the numbers showed (you can't be more basic than 1A!). As for the organisation of a complete unit to erect and staff a mobile station—well, that was just left to my imagination, and I soon felt that Yatesbury had little further attraction to me. I devised an escape plan.

The first stage was to telephone the adjutant at 60 Group HQ and explain that Yatesbury had said they had finished my revision course, so could I now leave? I had already learned that adjutants were busy people and often wielded far greater authority than their rank (usually flight lieutenant) warranted, for they sat in the outer office of the station commander and basked in the sunlight reflected from the gold braid ("scrambled egg" we called it) adorning the Great Man's cap.

As I hoped, the adjutant said "yes". Before he had time for second thoughts, I shot off to see the adjutant at Yatesbury and told him I had instructions from Group HQ to proceed at once on embarkation leave. Ten minutes later I was out of camp and away, on foot, lugging a suitcase and loaded down with greatcoat, gas mask and steel helmet.

It was mid-afternoon on December 4 and I had 40 miles across country to do. Four hours, three lifts and a lot of walking later, I found myself in Frome on a cold, dark, damp night. There were no trains, no buses, no cars, no street lights, no house lights—nothing for it but to start walking, up the hill out of the valley. My suitcase got heavier with every step, but eventually, just as I was thinking of returning to the town to try to find a bed for the night, an old car came chuckling up the hill behind me. I waved frantically into the tiny light escaping from the hoods fastened to the headlights and the driver stopped.

He seemed a bit suspicious at first, possibly with the thought of German parachutists but more probably because he was a farmer using petrol on a journey of doubtful legality, so I explained who I was and where I wanted to go and added knowledge of the local countryside to allay his suspicions. He took me to the outskirts of Mere, where once again I found myself alone on a country roadside

By now it was past 10 o'clock, with no possible hope of another lift and still four miles from home. Nothing for it but to start walking again, with stops every quarter of an hour to shift gas mask and webbing to the other shoulder and suitcase to the other hand. That was a long, long four miles, but I reached home as midnight struck on the church clock.

The next 11 days were all mine, and no peremptory signals arrived from 60 Group to ask why I was not still at Yatesbury, so I was able to make the best of my extended seven-day pass. It was a thoughtful time for Peggy and me, since she alone knew that these days were my last in England for—for years, certainly; til the end of the war, probably; forever, possibly—but that remained an unspoken thought. No one must know of my impending journey overseas, for all troop movements were secret, and posters on every wall reminded us that "Careless talk costs lives" or, in lighter vein, "Be like Dad, keep Mum." Common self-

82

preservation was adequate spur to ensure one's silence, and I had no desire to be torpedoed in mid-Atlantic.

We still had a little petrol for the Austin 7 as the pharmacy was regarded as essential, and this enabled us to visit our favourite local haunts for a nostalgic reminder of times of peace. Sadly, Windmill Hill at East Knoyle, where 18 months ago we had shared a picnic, was scarred and burnt by the remains of a Spitfire which seemed to have flown straight into the hillside. Silently, we stood among the scattered debris and thought of the pilot, so recently young and alive like us, whose blood now stained the tangled aluminium at our feet.

On Sunday Peggy and I shared the back seat of the tiny Austin while my parents drove us to Cheddar. We lunched in the Bath Arms and then walked in the gorge, silent and deserted and still unspoiled by souvenir shops. At the cave entrance stood a sentry ("ammunition dump?" I wondered), who sprang to attention, shouldered arms and accorded me the prescribed rifle-butt salute.

I saluted back, feeling very grown-up and important, while within I was toying with the childish temptation to go a bit further up the gorge and then discharge my Colt automatic, just to hear the echo reverberating around the cliffs. We were indeed children at heart—but children suddenly plunged into a grown-up world of war and death and lovers' partings.

Bruce with Peggy and mother

Saturday December 14 brought the last day of my official leave and news of my promotion to acting flight lieutenant, which meant an increase in pay to the dizzy heights of 19 shillings a day, so Peggy and I went to Salisbury to buy the braid so that she could sew my two white rings on each sleeve to replace the single half-width ring of a pilot officer.

We also lingered outside a jeweller's window while we debated whether or not to buy an engagement ring, which she would have had to wear secretly on a ribbon round her neck. To do so openly was quite unthinkable for a girl who was still at school, even though she was 17 years old. In the end, we decided against, for we knew our minds and needed no outward signal.

RAF Uxbridge, where I reported the next day, had been built in peacetime as the No 1 Depot of the Royal Air Force with a massive parade ground and solidly built barracks blocks, now supplemented by the inevitable wooden huts. Here, troops were assembling for dispatch overseas and there was a general area of disorder and bewilderment, with much issuing of kit and checking of nominal roles.

I eventually found that I was to command No 258 MRU, which stood for Mobile Radio Unit but which had to be described as 258 AMES for security reasons. There was no chance to meet any of the men before I was sent off again on leave, with strict orders to report back to Uxbridge on Christmas Eve. At least this would give me another week at home, and on my way through London I made an unofficial call on the Air Ministry to see my former CO from Worth Matravers, now a squadron leader behind a Whitehall desk. He could give me only a few minutes' time and no information as to my future, so I made my way on foot across the blacked-out Hungerford Bridge to the dimly lit Waterloo station, from where the familiar 6 o'clock train soon puffed and snorted its way into the night, to reach Gillingham on schedule at 8.18 pm.

No-one was expecting me and curiously nobody seemed surprised at my extra leave, nor did they suspect that this meant overseas, so Peggy (who alone shared my secret) and I were able to spend a few happy and nostalgic days in visits to our local familiar haunts of summers past—to Duncliffe Hill, Penselwood and Stourton Lake and to walks across the Chantry fields and across the meadows to the old oak.

I left my departure until the very last train on the night of December 23, and a cold, bleak night it was as we stood on the platform and waited and waited. Perhaps there was an air raid on Exeter or Plymouth? A whole hour went by and we just stood, with nothing left to say; torn between thankfulness for just a few minutes more together and the wish that the wretched train would come and we would get the parting over and done with.

At last we could feel, rather than hear, the rumble of the distant engine, well before its one dim oil lamp flickered into sight. I took leave of my mother and father, who retreated to the back of the platform as the train drew in and left us alone for a last wordless embrace at the carriage door. I was the only passenger, and seconds later, as the train gathered speed, my last glimpse of the forlorn little figure on the platform vanished behind the cloud of steam which always bounced back from the railway bridge on the Shaftesbury Road.

I shall never know what time the train reached Waterloo, but it was 4 am when I woke, in the silent, still compartment, shivering with cold, to find that I was the only occupant of the train and the platform.

In search of light and warmth, I walked down the stationary escalator into the underground, although the first trains were not due for some time. It was a shock, not so much the sight of every square foot of platform and corridor filled with huddled, sleeping figures, but the stench which rose from such a mass of humanity and hit me like a blow in the face. This was the height of the air raids, and bedrolls were staked out from dusk as Londoners almost fought to secure a place to lie on the unyielding concrete. Once the last train had run, there was no movement of air in the whole underground system, for ventilation is provided only by the trains pushing air along in front of them. More than that, the tunnels adjacent to the Thames all had watertight doors shut during the night air raids in case of flooding.

Despite the smell, the relative warmth of the underground was preferable to the bleak mainline station, so I sat on my suitcase on the edge of the platform to wait for the first train to Uxbridge and breakfast in the mess.

On Christmas Eve I met my adjutant, Flying Officer Tolman, a quiet, pleasant fellow just twice my age, and I had a first glimpse of some of the 50 assorted airmen who comprised my command. There was little enough of Christmas festivity about the place, and December 25 was just another working day. In fact, on Christmas Day itself I was sent up to the Air Ministry, together with the CO of another MRU forming at Uxbridge, to see a certain group captain who hinted darkly that we probably would not be going overseas at all.

It seemed that a struggle was going on in the Air Ministry between those who wanted to strengthen the defence of the British Isles and those who wanted to carry on the war against Germany in North Africa. While therefore we were currently meant to go to Egypt and on to Malta and Greece, we were warned that this might change, and I was personally told that I might expect to go to Scapa Flow.

This state of indecision filled the next few days. So far as the issue of kit was concerned, it still appeared that we were being prepared for dispatch to the Middle East, when on December 30 we CEOs were suddenly dispatched to the Air Ministry to report to Group Captain Lang, the uncle of my friend Norman Hughes. He told us that we were to go to Egypt in a troop convoy, but first we were to report to Kidbrooke to see our equipment which was being prepared there for separate shipment.

So on the very last day of 1940 we took the train across London, past the smoking ruins left by last night's bombing, for a brief visit to the depot. All we in fact saw were a few lorries standing in the yard; there was no time at all to familiarise ourselves with any of the equipment or take responsibility for the million-or-so-pounds' worth of radar which was now our responsibility, but we were each given our personal set of secret documents, printed on special thin paper, which must never be allowed to fall into enemy hands.

There were no boxes, destructor, lead-lined, full of sulphuric acid on board troopships, so I suppose we were expected to eat these papers as a last resort.

We left Kidbrooke promptly after lunch, to get "home" to Uxbridge in daylight. That night there was a dance in the mess to see the New Year in, but this was of little interest to me, with no partner, so I just ate the buffet supper, sang "Auld Lang Syne" and went to bed, wondering what 1941 would hold in store.

***

I was allowed out of Uxbridge just once more, on January 2, up to 18.00 hours, so I went by train to Watford, where I called on my school friend Ronald Kennedy and his now aged parents. (This was the last time we were to meet: sadly, although he survived the war, he later died from shotgun wounds after a back garden dispute with a neighbour.) I also called on my former headmaster, Edward Reynolds, so my last day in England passed in social visits.

All next day we were on standby. It was only after dark when troop movements started: columns of airmen were marched out of barracks to the railway station, with

NCOs in front and at the rear carrying hurricane lanterns. As officers, we had the privilege of riding in trucks to the station, where we were piled into the first-class carriages. We sat and waited, in the dimmest of lighting and with no heat, until at last the train set off, bound for we knew not where.

It was impossible to sleep. The bitter cold penetrated my greatcoat, hour after hour as the train alternately ambled along or stopped for long periods, always away from any stations. I suppose we were being kept "somewhere in England" and away from cities and ports, while the night air raids were on, and soon after dawn the wisdom of this became apparent. We drew slowly into a siding and, peering out, I could see snow on the ground, while on the next track was a goods train with its trucks on fire from enemy bombing. We were in Liverpool docks.

Any ocean liner viewed from the quayside is an impressive sight, but I had never before seen any ship at close quarters, and as I walked across the rail tracks to the *Duchess of Richmond* I was staggered at the sheer size of the steel wall towering above me. All was hurry and bustle as several thousand men were poured into the vessel, to be crammed into every inch of below-decks space amid a welter of kit bags, hammocks, gas masks and steel helmets, while the dockside cranes clanked and swung their loads into the holds.

Each airman had just enough space to swing a hammock in the mess deck where he would eat and live, elbow to elbow with his mates, for the next nine weeks. As officers we were luxuriously treated by comparison, although every two-berth cabin was double-bunked to take four of us, with room for only one at a time to wash and dress.

All that day and the next, a Sunday, were filled with the continuous arrival of more troops and stores, until the poor *Duchess* was bursting at the seams. No doubt the port authorities were anxious to be rid of us, and the thought of one bomb landing on such a concentrated mass of humanity as we now had, crowded below decks—well, we just didn't like to think of it.

Happily (or perhaps by design) it yet had a week to go before the next full moon and no further night raids took place while we were in Liverpool, but certainly there seemed to be some delay in getting to sea. It was Monday January 6 before we were warped out through the massive lock gates, to spend yet another night at anchor in the dangerous Mersey River. At dawn we at last seemed to set out, but a few hours later were at anchor again, in sight of land, lying off Anglesey. Here we waited for three days before sailing across the Irish Sea to anchor in Belfast Loch, waiting for darkness. Midnight saw us underway once more but cruising slowly and still alone.

Sunday January 12 saw me on deck at dawn as we cruised past the Mull of Kintyre and Ailsa Craig, out into the cold North Atlantic. The reason for our devious startings and stoppings of the last eight days soon became clear as we began to converge on other ships, from other ports, to form up into a massive flotilla.

There were several other troopships, including our twin, the *Duchess of Bedford*, and numerous cargo vessels, all keeping their station in a seemingly meticulous pattern, covering many square miles of ocean. Around the outside an escorting screen of destroyers fussed backwards and forwards at high speed, and our flanks were protected by cruisers. In the middle, looking surprisingly small compared with the troopships because of her lower profile, and keeping station like the merchantman, was the battleship *Ramilles*. In a sense we were protecting her against a torpedo attack while she was there to protect us against the awful havoc which could be caused by an enemy battleship.

There was a great deal of signal traffic between the ships and the naval escort with Aldis lamps flashing from bridge to bridge. Every now and again, but not at precisely timed intervals, the whole massive convoy would change course, as we zigzagged our way further and further north and the sea got colder and colder.

I endeavoured to keep some personal check on our navigation, as the thought was always there that at any moment, almost, one might find oneself clinging to a life raft or swimming in the sea. Longitude was impossible, but latitude could be determined to the nearest degree by means of a paper protractor and a sight of the Pole Star. I knew we were taking a huge sweep northwards and westwards out into the Atlantic and nearly to Iceland; daily I persisted in my cold bath, in seawater pumped straight up from the Arctic Circle in January, in the hope that this toughening against shock might give me just a few more minutes of survival if I had to swim for it. I also kept bars of chocolate and my Colt .455 in the pocket of my greatcoat by the cabin door (which was never, ever closed). Each cabin door had a latch which would secure it open by a few inches, with the idea that a normally shut door could be jammed tight by distortion of the cabin framework when a torpedo struck.

All this sounds pathetic now, but it was real enough at the time and there was no need for discipline to enforce the rule that everyone on board had to carry a life jacket with him at all times.

I always tried to be on deck before dawn as this was when things happened. One such morning, I scanned all round and found, to my surprise, that *Ramillies* had disappeared. Unaccountable shipboard rumour soon decided that she had detached to Gibraltar with some of the escort.

On another morning I found the convoy slowed to half speed and all flags at half-mast as one of the troopers conducted a burial at sea. The story soon circulated that the burial was because someone had cut partly through the hammock rope of a soldier who had broken his neck in the fall—but whether this was true or just circulated as propaganda to warn the troops of the danger of such a prank, we never knew.

***

Dawn on January 25 suddenly saw us translated into a new world, for we were entering Freetown Harbour in Sierra Leone, and our ship was surrounded by canoes full of boatmen and boys who would dive for coins. (At least, they would dive for silver coins but not copper, and so the troops wrapped pennies in silver paper and marvelled at the flow of foul language which even the smallest boy could let loose when the spluttering negro surfaced and found he had been tricked.)

Mid-morning there was a sudden air raid alarm. As we flocked down to the lower decks, the AA guns all opened up around us and a solitary aeroplane flew overhead, apparently a Vichy-French aircraft from Dakar, reporting our arrival to the Germans.

We spent four days at anchor, hot and airless in the tropical heat of the White Man's Grave, West Africa, and my thoughts went back to my brief interview with Unilever. Still, the green shoreline of the harbour looked attractive,

92

and we RDF officers somehow got permission to go ashore "to visit the secret Air Ministry Experimental station".

This was a masterly piece of wangling, for none of the other troops were allowed ashore; nor did we ever get to see the station, but the local CO did meet us for a drink in "the best hotel in Freetown" (which was probably also the second worst) and we had a chance to walk on dry land. Looking back, the trip was a foolhardy one, for none of us had been inoculated against yellow fever and we should never have been allowed ashore.

The next dawn treat was on February 8, when far to the north on the horizon was the quite unmistakeable outline of Table Mountain. But we were not for the Cape and sailed on, until three days later we made a new landfall at Durban. The brilliantly lit seafront city was a memorable sight after the so-strict onboard blackout, and here we were to lie alongside with all troops free to go ashore.

Durban was the most English of the South African cities, and South Africa was still then part of the British Empire. Their hospitality was staggering. All British troops were free to travel without payment on the buses, but there was no need for this concession—the inhabitants queued up in their cars at the quayside to offer unlimited free trips and free meals to any servicemen.

Thus I was taken on a tour of Umhlaga and the Valley of a Thousand Hills by someone who would only say his name was Bill, and I dined each night in the home or hotel of some stranger anxious to give hospitality. The wife of one of these, Mrs Musgrove, promised to write to Peggy after we had left and say that I was alive and well; long afterwards I learned that she had kept her word. (By this time I had been away from home for seven weeks

93

incommunicado, so any tenuous contact was to be seized upon.)

We now had 12 days at sea, all out of sight of land, as we ploughed our way northwards in the relative safety of the Indian Ocean. Mostly, I slept on deck in a hammock, to enjoy the cool night air and the incomparable view of the stars which the strict blackout permitted, with the Southern Cross dominating the constellations in place of the more familiar Plough and Cassiopeia in the northern hemisphere. But the darker the night, the brighter was the phosphorescence stirred up by the bow wave, bright enough to see the flying fish breaking the surface and the new splashes of light as they hit the waves a hundred yards away.

We made what we could of the limited space to give the troops sport and recreation, and I found myself taking up boxing again under an RAF corporal PT instructor known as Benny Sharkey, who had been a world-class professional fly-weight. Boxing had never been my favourite sport, but rather I forced myself into it to get used to being knocked out without losing my temper, and because any extra skill can always be useful in an emergency.

Here was a chance to learn from a real pro, and Benny was a great character. He would spar with anyone of any weight, using his speed to keep out of trouble and, although now much above his class weight, he really was amazingly fast. "Hit me," he would say as, with his guard lowered, he swayed around on his heels like a tumble-puppy.

Hit him I did, just once (when I followed up a feint more quickly than he expected) smack on the nose. I had only a split second to register the surprise in his eyes before one! two! his counterattack sent me reeling; but even then he hit me only hard enough to teach me a lesson when he could undoubtedly have laid me flat, and I have never forgotten the lesson of his total self-control. Thank you, Benny Sharkey.

On 27 February we steamed into Aden harbour, and a pretty uninviting place it looked, surrounded by barren, jagged, volcanic rocks. We left the same day, plying up the Red Sea and here, away on the port hand, could be seen a low smudge of land which we knew was a part of Africa still held by the Italian enemy. It was a strange feeling to look at enemy territory, as we sailed unconcernedly past.

The ship must have collected dispatches at Aden, for I was told by the orderly room that I had been gazetted as a War Substantive Flying Officer. This meant that if I lost my acting rank as flight lieutenant, I should not have to revert back to pilot officer. It also meant that somebody in the Air Ministry not only knew that I was still alive but actually knew where I was!

Chapter 7

Egypt

On March 3, two whole months after leaving Uxbridge, we dropped anchor in Port Tewfik at the southern end of the Suez Canal. Five whole days we waited, through rumour and counter rumour about disembarkation, until finally lighters appeared alongside, baggage was swung out and we were on our way to the sights and smells of Egypt. Port Tewfik does not boast much in the way of sites (apart from the red rock mountains that make a backdrop to the desert), but it certainly makes up for it with the smells.

A long, hot, slow train journey took us to Abu Sueir, a pre-war RAF station a few miles from Ismailia, which was itself a French-style colonial town on Lake Timsah, halfway up the canal. Abu Sueir had a proper officers' mess and I had a proper officer's room all to myself, but above all it had freshwater baths! One has to spend nine weeks aboard a troopship with only salt water to wash in to appreciate the joy of lying in a bath full of hot, fresh water.

There was nothing much to do at Abu Sueir, for although I was still CEO of 258 MRU my airmen were looked after under the SWO (the station warrant officer who, on every large station, was a trifle higher than God to every other rank and who held a great deal more power than a mere acting flight lieutenant). I opened a bank account at Barclays DC&O in Ismailia, to which my allowances could be credited, and I also started a rudimentary filing system with the help of my corporal clerk CD, but this was only playing at running my own unit and I knew it.

Abu Sueir, however, did have aeroplanes, and I soon got to know one of the maintenance test pilots.

"Sure," he said, "I'll take you up. Get a parachute out of stores. I'm just going up in a Blenheim," and as casually as that, my very first flight was fixed.

A sergeant strapped me, as tightly as possible, into the parachute harness. "This is the ripcord," he said, "and there's only one thing to remember. If you're falling to earth and you can't find it, open your eyes and look for it. I've seen bodies on the tarmac with the clothes clawed off, trying to find a ripcord which was there all the time."

With that friendly advice ringing in my ears, I climbed into the upper gun turret which gave the best view, and we thundered off into the sky. This was a short-nose Blenheim, adapted as a fighter bomber (rather than the medium bomber role of the long-nose version) and had wing-mounted forward-firing machine guns. After climbing well above the clouds and doing the necessary checks, my pilot, perhaps for my benefit, did some ground strafing out in the desert wastes, diving down at an alarming angle with machine guns blazing, to pull out at about 100 feet while my stomach continued on down into the sand and my ears rang with the din of gunfire.

A few days later I organised another free pleasure flight. I learned that a school friend, Peter Harvey, was at Shallufa, down the canal, and when I spoke to him over the service telephone he borrowed his CO's Miles Magister and flew over to Abu Sueir on a visit. The "Maggie" was a single-engine trainer with two open cockpits, and I soon took to the idea of "real" flying as we climbed over the desert with the wind in our hair and Peter did a few tight turns to show me what a light aircraft was like, compared with the heavy bombers which he flew on operations.

He called out through the voice pipe, "Keep your straps on, I'm going to do a loop," and we went into a dive to get up speed and then shot up—and up—and up—and then past the vertical. Clearly there was not enough power or momentum to maintain the 1-plus G necessary to get over the top, so two inevitable things happened simultaneously: a choking mass of desert sand fell out of the voice pipe into my face, and we went into a spin as the Maggie stalled and began to spiral earthwards.

Peter, of course, knew what to do, and while I was still wondering where the horizon had gone, it suddenly popped into view, reasonably straight and level and in front again. Perhaps not wanting to bend the CO's aircraft, Pilot Officer P.G.A. Harvey prudently decided not to try again, and we coasted back to the airstrip.

Here, after twice going around ("much better than making a bad landing", said Peter) we landed safely and repaired to the mess for a glass of Egyptian beer (which always tasted of onions) and lunch.

At this time the war seemed pretty remote, and North Africa was officially still only occupied by nothing worse than Italians, but stories soon came to us, from aircrew who had returned from the desert, of seeing enormous troop concentrations of Germans.

It was the Germans, too, who now tried to mine the Suez Canal—and with some success. One night one of the mines they dropped from aircraft hit the land and detonated, making a pressure wave which we felt from 10 miles away. The effect, as it spread across Abu Sueir camp, could be monitored by the clanging of the massive hangar doors as, at the speed of sound, the pressure reached each hangar in turn.

By this time, we knew all about magnetic mines, and the canal was soon judged to be swept, but the cunning enemy won this round. In the narrow waters of the canal they used a "notch-up" device so that the first few magnetic impulses received (whether from ships passing or from magnetic sweeps) only clicked on a counter—until the nth impulse blew up an unsuspecting ship and the canal was blocked.

Mines or no mines, Lake Timsah, through which the Suez Canal ran, was splendid for sailing, and with nothing else to do I spent several happy days with a hired sailboat. By simply crossing the lake one could sail from Africa to Asia. Moored in the lake was King Farouk's royal yacht, under armed guard, but this did not stop us from sailing up to it and chatting to the sentries.

A dhow

During this enforced holiday I made repeated efforts to find out why we were so idle, and all the information I could gather indicated that the slow cargo convoy which had been supposed to bring our equipment direct to Egypt had been attacked by the Germans and our precious "mobile radio units" sent to the bottom. This was later denied, but the denial was probably just for security reasons and I tended to believe, as later proved to be the case, that I should never again see my command.

As events proved, the loss of my equipment probably saved my life and certainly saved my liberty, for I learned that 258 MRU had been intended to go to Crete, which was soon to fall to the German airborne assault with the loss or capture of almost all the British forces on the island. (Stragglers who escaped to Egypt were reported as saying that the Germans had captured one radar unit and stuck the crew to it with bayonets, like butterflies to a specimen box; but it was never possible to tell the truth from rumour, nor propaganda from counter-propaganda.)

The end of March brought me my very first news of any sort from home, in the form of a cable simply saying, "all is well", but it was another fortnight until the first precious letters arrived, written early in January and posted while I was still at anchor off Anglesey.

To celebrate, I obtained a 48-hour pass and went by train to Cairo with a friend, one Flying Officer Nevitt. We stayed in the Continental Hotel and did the rounds of the tourist circuit, including a climb to the top of Cheop's pyramid and to the top of the flagpole on its summit. We also went up the sloping tunnel to the very centre of the pyramid, to the King's burial chamber, and felt the pressing claustrophobia of the thousands of tons of stone piled over us. We climbed all over the Sphinx, too, and then repaired to the Mena House Hotel (where later Winston Churchill was to go for his conference) and swam in the pool.

Cheop's pyramid

The Sphinx

The waiting dragged on through April, relieved only by a trip of a few days which I wangled to go to Aboukir on "temporary duty" at an RDF commanded by John Ratcliffe, who had been a friend of mine at Cambridge. We celebrated our reunion with a dinner at the Union Club in Alexandria, and I had a chance to see an MRU actually working, although I spent much of the time swimming in the Mediterranean.

The train journey back to Abu Sueir was highly unpleasant, involving a whole day of discomfort with a four-hour halt among the dirt and smells of Benha, so when I had the chance a few days later of road transport to Cairo, I grabbed it and went (I suppose technically I was absent without leave) to try to find out why I had nothing to do.

I actually found my way into HQ RAF Middle East and saw the chief radio officer (the head of the still-secret RDF organisation), but the most he could offer was the probability that when he had any equipment I would

101

probably be sent with my crew of 238 MRU to Beni Suef. This was, I learned, some 200 miles south of Cairo, up the Nile, and the idea was to provide early warning cover against a flanking air attack from the south. Meanwhile, I had better get back to Abu Sueir!

Happily, in the outer office I found John Findlay whom I knew from Queens' College days as a fellow physicist. He was a civilian boffin in the same business, attached to HQME, and he gave me a night's accommodation in his flat.

Next day, May Day, I set out early to try and get back to Abu Sueir before I was found out. The airfield at Heliopolis was worth a try and I went around the flights and orderly rooms in the hope of an aircraft going down to the canal: no luck. The only hope was a lift in military transport, and eventually this worked after some walking through the suburbs.

I got safely back before I was missed. I was just in time to say goodbye to my adjutant, Flying Officer Tolman, who had been posted that morning to Palestine and was hitching a lift in a Wellesley bomber which happened to be taking off in the right general direction. This looked like the beginning of the end of my command and was also a warning to me that I too might suddenly be missed if I kept on wandering about Egypt without permission.

For my next outing I arranged an official visit to 204 AMES on the seashore at Damietta, which meant driving a station wagon down the canal to Port Said and then literally along the beach, at the low tide line, to the tip of the delta. The day I made this trip, Hitler's deputy Rudolph Hess was on an outing of his own—flying across the North Sea to parachute into Scotland. He has been in jail ever since.

I continued prodding away at HQME about something to do, and by some means the adjutant got to hear of it. I was hauled into his office and was severely rebuked for telephoning Cairo without his permission.

"Why not?" I said. "I am the CO of my own unit and only staying on your station."

He looked pretty grim and sent me packing, but very soon after we birds of passage were dispatched from Abu Sueir and began a new life at Kasfareit, in a huge tented camp in the desert close to the Great Bitter Lakes, further down the canal towards Tewfik. This was known as MEP or more fully as the Middle Eastern Pool and was a sort of transit camp for personnel they didn't know what to do with.

As there was plenty of labour, including many Italian POWs, the practice was to dig huge holes in the sand and then erect the tents five feet below ground level, which was pretty sensible seeing what damage a fragmentation bomb could do to an unprotected square mile of tents full of sleeping troops. As we were posted to MEP this meant the tacit death of my own 258 MRU, and I began to wonder if I should keep my two rings as an acting flight lieutenant, when no longer filling a flight lieutenant's establishment. On the whole it seemed best to keep my mouth shut and keep my two rings up, so I did just that.

There was even less to do at Kasfareit than at Abu Sueir, and after a morning censoring mail I hitched a lift down to Shallufa, an operational aerodrome some 15 miles south, where I made a call on Peter Harvey. Peter was in bed having spent the last night flying to Greece on a bombing mission; there was still a war going on for some. Indeed, the war suddenly took a new turn when on 22 June Germany invaded Russia.

***

Six weeks passed with nothing to do except censor the mail which the equally bored troops turned out in sacksful. I managed a couple of unofficial trips to Ismailia, where I was smuggled into the RAF mess for free meals by some Australian aircrew friends, and two trips to Cairo and back.

One of these was official, so I called on HQME in another attempt to try to get a job. Maybe this was a mistake, for I was told I was to be sent to Aden as soon as transport was available. Perhaps, if I had kept my head down, I should have avoided this posting to perhaps the most unpopular Service station in the whole world, but it was too late now, and I went back to Kasfareit to await my fate.

The RAF had a curious habit of sending me in the wrong direction, and rapidly orders came that I was to move to Aboukir. The appointed day for this was July 5, and it seemed that I was the only officer going on a special train containing some 250 other ranks, so naturally I became OIC train, charged with the responsibility for getting the troops safely to the Mediterranean coast.

We paraded at dawn, all with webbing and haversack rations (the "unexpended portion of the day's ration" in the official jargon) and entrained in dilapidated coaches crammed full of men, behind a puffing steam engine that seemed incapable of more than 20 miles an hour—and that interspersed with many stops. I rode in the last coach, sweating at an open window and trying to keep an eye on my charges during the stops to see that no one got left behind, for of course the men hopped out whenever the train stopped, in search of air and bladder relief.

We wandered, in zigzag fashion, across the sands of the delta, all day and far into the night. Just before dark there was a most alarming incident when we were steaming at walking pace through the station of an Egyptian town, lined with Arabs who looked none too friendly.

Sitting on the step at the front of my end carriage was an airman smoking a pipe, and just as he passed the end of the platform a native snatched the pipe out of his mouth and ran off. The airman, quick as a flash, hopped down onto the track, ran back to the platform, grabbed his pipe, threw a punch at the startled Arab and then tried to catch us up as we slowly gathered speed. I leaned out of the window as far as I could, shouting encouragement, as he disappeared from my view behind the rear of the carriage to run the better at the centre of the track. There was no communication cord, and anyway to stop the train might have meant a full-scale riot, so all I could do was to hope for the best.

I was just beginning to feel confident, for our speed was still modest, when, looking down, I perceived that we were crossing a river bridge with ominous gaps down to the muddy water between each sleeper. What sort of court-martial would I get for losing an airman, either drowned or savaged by a mob?

Happily, at our next unscheduled stop he turned up, smiling, having just scrambled onto the tail end of the coach and clung on before the gaps in the sleepers were reached, so I was able to deliver my full quota of men when we finally drew into Aboukir at 2 o'clock next morning, tired, hungry, sweaty and dirty.

For me there was no room in the mess and I found myself billeted out in the New Victoria Hotel in the village, where a few other officers from other services were lodged. This hotel had only about a dozen rooms but was run by a Frenchman, so the food was good and on the whole my stay there was pleasant. The sea was only 50 yards away, so we could swim and sunbathe all day while we waited for something to happen. There was not long to wait.

That evening, just as we were finishing dinner, an air raid warning sounded, and it soon became apparent that an attack on Alexandria was underway, so we all trooped up on to the flat roof of the hotel to see the fun. This vantage point was a little higher than the roofs of the surrounding native houses which comprised the village of Aboukir and commanded a view both out to sea and across the neighbouring RAF base to Alexandria itself.

All along the coast and around Alexandria Harbour searchlights probed and swept the skies, now and again focussing into a cone as they caught a target, and then the ack-ack opened up, with the deep-throated hollow boom of the heavies mingled with the more rapid and staccato fire of the Bofors. Seen from a safe distance, the tracer shell seemed to rise so slowly, climbing delicately into the night sky like a slow-motion firework display.

As the raid developed and more gunfire came from the defensive ring around Aboukir base, one of the bright sparks among us (we were a mixed bag of RAF, Fleet Air Arm and army officers) thought of joining in, but small arms fire against high-level bombers is not much use and no German parachutist seemed to be dropping in our vicinity, so for want of anything better to shoot at he tried the idea of seeing how effective our steel helmets were against bullets, by propping his tin hat on the parapet and blasting away at it with a Smith and Wesson .38, the spent bullets winging their way across the native village or ricocheting off the parapet.

It seems that a glancing bullet would make a healthy dent in, but not quite penetrate, the issue steel helmet and one foolhardy individual volunteered to wear his helmet and be shot at, but happily no one else was prepared to do the firing. The anti-aircraft firing died away and we all went down to the bar as the all-clear sirens sounded, but that was by no means the end of the affair.

Into the hotel suddenly burst a very angry assistant provost marshal (APM) bearing the rank of squadron leader and the authority of the combined chiefs of staff of the whole Allied command. It seemed that a sentry at the nearest compound gate between the base and our village had reported gunfire coming from the New Victoria Hotel, and I suppose the authorities always had to have in mind the possibility of fifth column activity among the Egyptians, so they did not welcome unauthorised gunfire from the heart of a native village.

I do not know what action was taken by the other services, but as far as the RAF was concerned next morning brought a peremptory order in DROs (daily routine orders): "All Officers billeted in the NVH are to hand in their revolvers to the station armoury forthwith."

Now here was a problem, for I had no intention of parting with my gun, and anyway I still had my "Secret and Confidential" publications to defend, even though my old 258 MRU seemed to have been dissolved. I was debating with myself whether I could plead a special case, when I suddenly thought of a bright idea—do nothing.

106

"Me? ... I've never been issued with a revolver" would be my answer if called to account, since in all logic my .455 Colt automatic pistol certainly did not revolve and the order clearly stated "revolvers". So I sat tight, kept my counsel to myself, kept my gun locked up in my trunk and never heard any more about it.

***

Four weeks passed—unpleasant, if boring, idleness, when the only official duty I had to perform was a continuous 24 hours guard to a young pilot officer who had been put under close arrest awaiting court-martial.

But I did get in some more flying, with the Fleet Air Arm this time. Sub Lieutenant O'Flynn let me fill the observer's seat in his Fulmar fighter for a squadron training exercise which included formation flying, aerobatics and a low-level beat-up of the landing strip, all exhilarating stuff.

A couple of days later I organised another flight with another FAA trainee, but I got no farther than sitting in the cockpit at the end of the runway, for when he tried to select Contact he pressed the wrong switch, there was a bang and the fire extinguisher flooded the engine with foam. Perhaps it was as well that that particular pilot never took my life in his hands.

Eventually, at 18.00 hours on August 2 came a warning signal to me to be ready to move to Aden, and by 20.00 hours I was on my way. It was just as well that I was in camp that evening, for I might well have been at dinner in Alex with a friend—another lucky escape!

I met, in the lorries taking us up to the railway station at Sidi Gaber, the detail of airmen who were to form my new command, and none of whom I had ever seen before. They roughly matched, in numbers and trades, the establishment for an MRU and had been snatched from their comfort, at an hour's notice and at the whim of the SWO, that evening. For a couple of hours, they sat in misery on the kit bags on the platform, waiting, like me, for a long-overdue

107

train, and when it finally chugged into the station it proved to be completely full of troops already. Each carriage bore a label "Reserved for RN" and all were full of sailors.

"You can't come in here, Sir," said a petty officer. "It's reserved, Sir".

I shoved him aside and shouted, "Who is in charge?"

After a moment's silence a burly chief petty officer, twice my age, indicated that he was but made no move from his corner seat. "This is reserved for us," he said. "You can't come in."

"Stand to attention when you are spoken to by an officer and call me 'Sir'." There was just a fraction of a second's delay, amid stunned silence from the carriage full of ratings, and then he climbed awkwardly to his feet.

"Move your men up to the other end. I'm putting my draft in this carriage. Now!" And without further ado the little confrontation was over, and soon men of both services were piled in together into every inch of gangway space, and the train chugged off.

It was another agonisingly slow journey up the delta until finally we reached Cairo at 6.15 am. The RTO, strangely, seemed to be aware of our transit, and within an hour we were entrained again for Port Tewfik. From there we were whisked away to the quayside and put on board a tender, which puffed out into the harbour while we looked anxiously around to see which ship we were bound for.

One by one, all the ships we thought were troopers slipped astern, until we were left with only one insignificant, smoky tramp steamer between us and the Indian Ocean. This was His Majesty's Troopship *Yoma*, looking too small to take our tender full of men, but she proved a comfortable little ship, for we were the only "passengers". I had a cabin to myself and messed with the other ship's officers.

It was unsafe to stay in Suez any longer than necessary, for the shipping was a prime target for the nightly raids, and we weighed anchor and sailed by sunset. This was just as well, for the radio that very night told us of 58 deaths from bombing in the port we had just left.

The following night another hundred died, but by that time we were 200 miles down the Red Sea. (Later in the war the *Yoma* was to be bombed and sunk by enemy action.)

The rest of that voyage was, for me, particularly unpleasant, for I spent 24 hours with most unpleasant diarrhoea, an infection known to the troops by various names such as Gyppy Tummy or Aden Gut or more usually as simply The Squitters, which I had probably caught from the flies which infested all the railway carriages.

No sooner had I struggled back to my feet after this than I was again in such agony of pain that I stumbled along to the MO's cabin at 2 am and collapsed screaming to the floor. Worthy man, he soon discovered that this was no connection with the dysentery but potentially more serious, for he guessed (rightly, it later proved) that I had a kidney stone lodged in the ureter.

Under any conditions this is one of the more painful experiences, but when the temperature is over 100 degrees and the humidity to match, with no air movement because the following wind matches the ship's speed, it is quite agonising. Whatever he doped me with, he managed to give me some relief, and the next morning I managed to pass the rock, with a good deal of blood as it scraped its way through, and a sense of relief which defies description.

The ship's doctor gave me a letter to the PMO at Aden and the cheering news that I might have to be sent home. Secretly I hoped that he was right, and I steamed open the letter to make sure he wasn't pulling my leg, but by the time we dropped anchor in Aden harbour I was feeling much better.

For 24 hours it was too rough to disembark, but on the morning of August 9 I managed to get ashore after a flying leap on to a tender, leaving all my kit and my airmen on board to wait for calmer seas.

Chapter 8

Aden

In the great days when the British fleet dominated the world, Aden was a vital coaling station, controlling the entrance to the Red Sea and the sea routes to India, Ceylon and the Far East. For no other reason could the British have ever wanted to colonise such a wholly uninviting spot. The harbour was flanked into the north and south by bare spiky mountains of igneous rock, the eroded remains of past volcanoes. To the northwest stretched flat desert for some 20 miles and to the southeast was the open sea.

The southern flank, "Little Aden", was devoid of human habitation, but around the base of the northern mountain peaks, on the harbourside, were clustered the native townships of fishermen, boatbuilders and goatherds, mingled with the services headquarters and military barracks.

All the water and food for this unprepossessing area had to come down from the hills inland, much of it by camel. Nothing grew—for there was no rainfall—except for a patch of grass at the governor's residence and a few trees which had to be watered. The whole of this area was dominated by the mountain of Shum-shum, the highest peak of the crater of the extinct volcano, and behind Shum-shum lay the ancient Arabic town of Crater, roughly where the original volcanic crater must have been.

Crater

Crater

From Shum-shum itself stretched out several ridges of rock, rather like the roots of a banyan tree, and one of these rose to its own peak, 1000 feet high, making a pinnacle which overhung the harbour entrance. Perched on the top of Aman Khal one could just see two aerial masts. I didn't know it as I stepped ashore, but this was to be my home.

Aden was an Air Force Command, for in pre-war days it was only by air that the tribes upcountry could be controlled. The aerodrome at Khormaksar was still using old biplanes, Hawker Harts, on bombing missions into the mountains, sometimes supported by RAF armoured cars, but there were a few Blenheims used for communication and coastal reconnaissance.

As it was, at this stage in 1941 Aden was something of a backwater compared with the fighting war in Egypt, and no more bombs had fallen on it for several months since the last Italian pilot who had made the attempt from Abyssinia had been shot down and captured. There was, I found, something of the relaxed, prewar, regular service life about Air Headquarters, where I soon found myself in the presence of the AOC.

Office hours seem to be from 6 am to 2 pm, after which the war stopped (as it seemed to me) until next day. It was all rather different from the 24-hour day and seven-day week which I had to come to regard as normal, back at home where the "real" war was on.

Next day I visited Aman Khal and found out just what I was in for. The first half of the way up was possible for wheeled transport by way of a dirt road carved out of the Knudsen-side, which wound its way up to the 500 foot level. The left side of this track fell away almost vertically to the valley bottom, and I was just working out how nasty it would be if the Adeni driver went too near the crumbling edge when, as if on cue, he stalled the engine. Unabashed, he started it again, put the vehicle in gear, revved up the engine till it screamed and let the clutch in with a bang.

The effect was dramatic alright, and the car leapt away—backwards! Happily, the driver did know his foot brake from his accelerator, even if he didn't know bottom from reverse, and we skidded to a halt on the edge of the precipice amid a cloud of dust and volcanic cinder. I got out, leaving the wretched man to try to force off the handbrake (I had pulled it on so hard that the ratchet was stuck), and walked to the top of the track where a little flatter space marked the end of the road. Above me rose another 500 feet of crumbling rock, negotiable only on foot by way of a zigzag path.

In normal times I rather like hillwalking, but when the temperature is over 100 degrees in the shade, and there isn't any shade anywhere, and the relative humidity is as near 100 percent as makes no difference, it was a sweaty job and no mistake.

At the top, surrounded by a masonry wall, was a concreted ribbon of steps from a higher to a lower level, the whole area being some 50 yards long and varying in width from a few feet to about 10 yards, within which were crammed the transmitter and receiver huts, plus a pair of wooden barracks huts with a tiny office and a guardroom. Here the crew of 240 AMES lived, slept and worked, with all their food, water, stores and petrol brought up to them on pack donkeys or carried by coolies. It was hard to imagine how the mass of concrete and stone and the radar equipment and power generators had been dragged up in the first place, but there it was.

The view was breathtaking, seaward to the sharp horizon at a distance of 40 miles, and then sweeping round, over Little Aden and the harbour, to the sandy wastes leading to the jagged mountains of Arabia, and round to the north, where the distant horizon was obscured by Shum-shum. Beneath lay the harbour installations of Aden with the service barracks and the native slums.

But on the first visit I had only a chance to meet Macey, whom I was to relieve, and have a brief look round before I had to return to enter hospital on the MO's orders. This was a pleasant three days of tests and x-rays while I wondered if I was to be sent home, and then I was declared fit and sent back to duty.

Next day a whole gang of coolies plodded up the path to the top of Aman Khal bearing my trunk and the airmen's kit bags, followed by my men and me, and in no time the outgoing crew had taken off and left us to fend for ourselves. I now had a unit to command again and a job to do, although it was not, it seemed, a very important one. (At one time Air Headquarters told me I need not keep 24-hour watches but provide cover only when they had aeroplanes flying out. This seemed to me to be so ridiculous, seeing that we were still theoretically within range of enemy held territory, that I ignored the order and still maintained full watchkeeping every hour of the day and night. I took my standards from the Battle of Britain, not from the peacetime wallahs who still lingered on in these remote commands.)

Naturally, with no enemy activity, we were able to devote some attention to making ourselves as comfortable as possible. There was an unlimited supply of native labour to do the cooking and dhobying, with a couple of low-caste untouchables to empty the latrines. I had my own servant, a jet-black African from Djibouti called "Frenchy" and each group of airmen had its own servant. An ordinary AC2 was, of course, a superior being in the eyes of a servant and was addressed as "Airman-sahib". I was, naturally, referred to as "Officer Sahib" and Frenchy was clearly at the top of the servant hierarchy.

As storekeeper we were fortunate to have LAC Jenkins who was in civvy street a Torquay hotelier and who took it on himself to see that we were the best fed unit in Aden and did it very well. Unhappily, the "meat" most freely available on ration was shark—grey, tough, leathery and tasting of cod-liver oil—but a stroke of luck came our way when we were all put on a special diet.

It happened this way: I had a routine visit from the MO and happened to discuss with him the possibility of our health being affected by sitting for hours in front of the cathode ray tube. A beam of electrons hitting a target was known to produce x-rays, and we just didn't know whether the glass screen was enough to protect us from this harmful radiation.

Like all doctors enthusiastic to make a new medical discovery, he promptly tested us all for anaemia and found, he thought, that our average blood count was low. As a precaution, he issued an order diverting all the available liver from Aden's meagre supply of slaughtered animals to our use—anything was better than shark!

***

For the rest, we just made ways of passing the time between watches. I made occasional visits down to the RAF mess at Tarshyne for a game of snooker with Jimmy Knowles (who had sailed with me aboard the *Yoma*) and for a swim in the Governor's pool, a special privilege for RAF officers.

This pool was just a portion of the harbour enclosed within a short net of wire mesh, rather like a sunken municipal tennis court, and it was a special thrill to swim here after dark on a pitch black, moonless night: One could feel one's way to the end of the springboard, plunge out into the darkness and, immediately on hitting the water, be bathed in brilliant flashes of green phosphorescence. The slightest disturbance of the water produced enough light to see by, and as our arms broke the surface they seemed to be dripping liquid fire, lighting our way back to the steps.

We swam here in daylight, too, and one day I was disconcerted to find a large underwater gap in the netting, after which I was a bit less keen, for sharks were not to be taken lightly. Two soldiers from a trooper in the harbour who had tried to swim ashore after being denied shore leave were just never seen again.

These brief visits to sea level were pleasant enough but were always spoilt by the need to climb back, on foot, to the top of my 1000-foot mountain. Even after dark, it was so hot and humid that one arrived back in a pool of sweat. Indeed, one sweated all the time, even sitting still, which called for a shower and freshly laundered clothing twice a day.

Both of these facilities were provided by the native servants. The shower was a four-gallon petrol tin with nail holes in the bottom, under which we stood while the bearer poured a gallon of precious water into the top. Clean khaki was always available, washed constantly by the dhobi-wallahs, who bashed it, wet, onto a stone until clean, dried it in the sun and then pressed it with an iron heated by glowing charcoal. With the aid of all this effort, one could be comfortable for about five minutes twice a day—longer than that and the sweat was once again soaking through shirt and shorts, leaving little puddles in the chair seats.

The administration of a simple unit such as I now commanded soon became a task that could be accomplished, with the help of Corporal Kenney (a southern Irish regular clerk GD), in a couple of hours daily. There was little enough air activity to make any operational demands on my time, so inevitably I fell to inventing things to pass the time.

Out of the meagre spares for the radar station I devised and constructed a telephone exchange to connect the individual huts on my mountaintop down to the civilisation below us known as Air Headquarters. Sometimes of an evening, when Jimmy Knowles had to sit in AHQ as duty

116

officer, waiting for the war to happen, he would call me up in my cabin on Ahman Khal and we would get out pencil and paper and play "Battleships"—anything to pass the time.

I acquired a radio, on which I could hear the BBC overseas news, relayed from the Aden transmitter and interspersed with the callsign "Dah-dah-dit-dit, dah-dit, dit-dah-dit, this is Station ZNR, Aden, Arabia". To hear the wartime announcers and listen to Vera Lynn singing "Yours" made England seem farther away than ever, for this instant communication was not for us simple servicemen.

I was now approaching the end of my third month without any mail from home, and this for the second time round, which seemed pretty hard. Then one day a whole batch of letters came in a bundle, having followed me down the Red Sea from Egypt, and I remember counting up the cost of the postage—nineteen shillings and seven pence—which was no mean sum of money in those days.

During this period the Airgraph letter was introduced which, if you had an address, speeded things up a bit. Your letter had to be written on one side of a standard form, which was then microfilmed and the negative flown back to England for printing and delivery at home. This whole process took only about two weeks, much better than ink and paper letters going by sea round the Cape.

As another diversion I improvised myself a lathe out of an electric motor to make a set of chessmen from the only wood available, which was the broken-up boxes (each box contained two tins) which came to us daily, by donkey or coolie, as our petrol supply and on which our whole operation depended. This lathe, being directly driven, whizzed around at the alarming rate of 1440 rpm, so it was highly dangerous if you let the chisel snag into the workpiece; but it was very effective and I have the chess set still.

I also exercised my troops in the defence of our mountain top, just in case a landing party from an enemy submarine should attempt to capture our secrets. As we had little in the way of guns, I made Molotov cocktails out of empty lemonade bottles and some of our precious petrol. It was very satisfying to hurl these from the Khud-side, after lighting a paraffin-soaked rag fuse, and see them explode in a sheet of flame.

I am sure my airmen thought me a little mad, and my senior officers in AHQ would probably, had they known, have court-martialled me for this unofficial initiative. But I was acutely aware of the importance of the secrecy of our radar system and also of the protection of my own skin, besides being disillusioned at the peacetime attitude of this outpost east of Suez. I did not know it then, but events were boiling up further east which would soon reshape my future and expose the weaknesses of our Far East presence.

Life began to assume something of an ordered pattern. Every dawn I would scan the horizon for shipping, mostly seeing nothing until (perhaps one morning out of every 30) the sea would be filled with ships as another convoy converged on Aden to refuel before the last leg of its long voyage to Egypt. On those days, all would be hustle and bustle in the harbour, with launches running errands from ship to ship and ship to shore, and tugs and barges everywhere, for large ships could not lie alongside.

Then, before sunset, they all sailed off again, and I would sit on the wall to watch their departure and stay to see the sun sink below the horizon, just like a penny in the slot, to be followed very swiftly by darkness as there is no twilight so near to the equator. Even on the non-convoyed days, I usually sat to watch the sunset from my mountaintop, for one of our few diversions every evening was to look down on the day's crop of funerals. We could see five cemeteries below us, and no corpses were ever kept unburied overnight, so there was always a funeral to watch.

Now and again it would be a service funeral and the bugle notes of the "Last Post" would reach up to us before night fell and (if, by luck, it was one of the rare days when there was a large beer ration) the troops would celebrate the departed with a sing-song. I was sometimes by invitation allowed to join in the other ranks' canteen on a beer night, for the RAF was much more advanced than the other two services in that quite a high degree of familiarity (off duty) seemed to be accepted—and without any loss of discipline or authority next morning.

Many traditional RAF songs were sung, through a beery haze but with great feeling. These mostly had their origins in the First World War but with updating and modification to take account of newer aircraft types, and with many local variations depending on the unit or command, or indeed the continent in which one happened to be serving.

Words of Arabic or Urdu were liberally interspersed with the usual profane English, laced with four-letter adjectives and plenty of wit, while in between the solos and the choruses came numerous traditional monologues and chants. I could write a book, from memory, giving hour after hour of these ballads, but they are best left to word-of-mouth handing down in the traditional way, and it is only because it was so symptomatic of the longing of the time-served overseas airmen that I give what was our version (to the well-known Irish melody) of "Roll on the Boat":

Sure, a little bit of mittI fell
From out the skies one day
And it landed in the ocean
Not so very far away.
And when the Air Force saw it,
Sure, it looked so f..... bare,
They said "That's what we're looking for,
We'll send the Air Force there."
So they sent out River Gun-boats, Armoured cars and SHQ,
And then they picked on TWO-FOUR-O
And sent out me and you
But peachey we'll be sailing.
To that land that's far remote
Until that day you'll hear me say
ROLL ON THAT F....... BOAT.

"Peachy-peachey" was a local word with a literal meaning of "soon" but having the implication that "soon" meant the tomorrow which was never meant to arrive, rather like the Spanish "mañana" but without the same sense of urgency. So "Peachey Peachy Tolo" was the name I gave to a puppy I acquired ("tolo" meant little) in a pathetic attempt to build something of a domestic life while I waited out the years until I could, in my turn, board that BOAT to take me home to begin life proper.

***

Peachey and I were soon to part, but for a few short weeks he scrambled with me over the Khud-side in the nearest substitute for a proper walk which I could give him. This was highly dangerous, for the loose lava crumbled away at a touch, and I went, unroped, into some very stupid situations.

On one occasion I felt hand- and footholds both beginning to slip simultaneously. I froze and sweated in the boiling sun, not daring to move and shaking at the thought of the jagged rocks which would receive me hundreds of feet below. Slowly, so slowly, I felt round with one hand for what seemed to be a better hold, and then, hardly daring to breathe, transferred a little of my weight, a bit at a time, to a safer position.

It was minutes before I dared move either foot, but somehow I sidled my way back to a more stable position where my puppy, despite his four-wheel-drive, had prudently waited. Later on, and from a safe position, I prodded this lump of Aman Khal with a crowbar, and two tons of rocks suddenly slid off into the void.

After that I left the eastern face severely alone but continued to explore the less precipitous southern slopes and thus discovered a cave, running right back into the mountain and containing thousands of bats which whizzed and screeched round one's head in great alarm.

Cave on the Khud

News came over the radio on December 7 of the Japanese attack on Pearl Harbor, and therefore the knowledge that we had, simultaneously, acquired a new and vicious enemy in the Far East and a new ally, America, in the Far West. It was a Sunday morning and everything seemed unchanged in Aden—no sirens sounded, there were no naval movements and our passive war went on its

121

unruffled way—and yet, we knew, it must catch up with us sooner or later.

Officially, nothing at all happened for two days, and then to my amazement I received over the telephone a signal from ministry to all unit commanders. It was prefixed MOST SECRET and told me that we were now at war with Japan. "Most secret" indeed, I thought. Was I allowed to tell my troops what they already knew? If I saw a Japanese aircraft approaching my mountaintop, was I allowed to shoot at it with my pistol, or should I shoo it away by waving the MOST SECRET signal at it?

On the surface, things in Aden went on just as before, and we set out to enjoy Christmas. LAC Jenkins surpassed himself in providing the whole unit with a splendid Christmas dinner, followed by a convivial evening centred around an extra beer ration, carefully hoarded for the occasion.

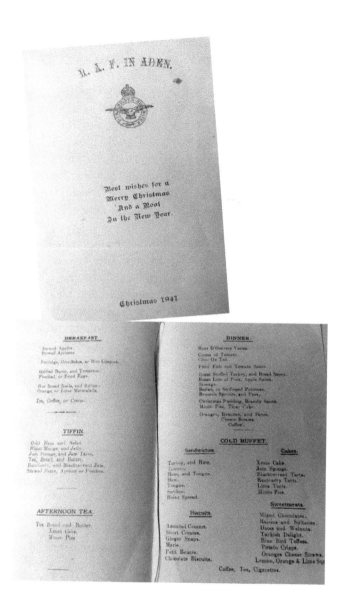

Christmas Menu

Unfortunately, this was too much for a certain Scottish NCO, who got drunk enough to be violent and went around smashing windows with his bare fists. When I was fetched he raised his fist to strike, and I had no course but to retreat, lest he did the unthinkable and ended up in jail for two years.

After a while he fell asleep on the canteen floor, where we left him until morning. Then, backed by a posse of the largest men in my unit, I woke him up and put him under close arrest. For one split second he had a wild gleam in his still partly inebriated eye, and I prepared to do a right swing—then, as sense and discipline crept back into his fuddled brain, he shambled awkwardly to his feet and was marched, under escort, down the mountains to the cells at SHQ.

I was magnanimous enough to charge him only with drunkenness, for "attempting to strike an officer" would have put him in jail and lost him his rank. Later on he thanked me most generously and we remained good friends, while I gained some respect from the other ranks for the way I had handled what had been, on our remote mountaintop, away from all other authority, a very tricky situation.

It was a lesson to me that discipline in an isolated command depends not so much on formal law as on the part of personality and mutual respect, a lesson which was to prove useful in the months ahead under far more dangerous circumstances.

On that Christmas day of 1941 the British forces in Hong Kong capitulated to the Japanese, while on Boxing Day our British Commandos made their first substantial raid, that on the Lofoten Islands in German-occupied Norway. British forces in the desert advanced to Benghazi, while the Americans, in Luzon, retreated to Manila. Everywhere (except, it seemed, in Aden) the war was getting faster and faster moving day by day, as the old year turned over and 1942 began.

There remains one singular event to record during my remaining few weeks on the barren rock. It rained, the first time for two years, and something like two inches fell in the space of an hour, flooding our hearts and pouring through the cracks in the sun-dried roofs until, as suddenly

124

as it started, it stopped, followed by the blazing sun and clouds of steam rising from the bare, baked rock.

What was even more remarkable, however, was the sudden crop of flowers that sprouted and grew over the whole Khud-side—and in a matter of hours, until they were 10 inches high and in full bloom. Three days later they had died, withered and gone, leaving the volcanic rock and dust as apparently barren as ever.

Presumably, in these few short hours, a new generation of seeds had fructified and fallen, to lie dormant, perhaps for years, till the next chance rainfall.

Sunday March 1 was a day to be remembered. It began with the sight of the monthly convoy from England streaming into harbour led by the *Pasteur*, one of the biggest liners afloat. We all lined the walls of our station, gazing at the ships which, we knew, had left England only six or seven weeks ago. We knew too that they would be bearing letters from home, probably with news as recent as last Christmas, but we could only guess which ship was carrying the mail, nor how long it would be before the precious letters reached our hands.

For me, those precious letters were to take another 16 days to my hands, and the reason was one of those enormous mess-ups that happened in wartime; this was the way of it.

Chapter 9

The wrong way up the Red Sea

At 11.00 hours the signal was relayed to me, through HQ Aden, from HQME in Egypt. This said, "80926 Flight Lieutenant B Samways posted to 272 AMES to command."

Where, or what, was 272 AMES? We did not know, but in the mind of Headquarters Aden, this signal meant only one thing: it was a chance to get one body off the ration strength, and one less mouth to feed was, it seemed, a very important thing.

So at noon I was given strict orders to embark by 14.00 hours that very day. This gave me only two hours to pack all my kit, dispose of my radio and dog, arrange coolies to carry my trunk down the mountain, collect my allowances to date from AHQ, turn over my command to my most senior NCO and walk down the track to the harbour. By 2 o'clock I left the quayside in the tender which had just brought the sacks of mail ashore (I must have been within feet of my expected letters) and boarded the *Pasteur* which promptly sailed for Egypt.

As she slipped out of the harbour, I stood on deck to watch the departure, to gaze up at Aman Khal and to wonder, as always, if I should ever set foot again in the place that had, despite all the discomfort, become the most permanent home I had had for a whole year. I thought too of the men I was leaving behind, who would I knew be watching my ship out of sight with envy, because I was going 1500 miles nearer to England.

I now had five days of idle luxury aboard the splendid ship with good meals served in the first-class saloon—and then once more I was back in Port Tewfik, dropped onto the quayside from a tender just like any other piece of luggage. The disembarkation officer did not of course have me on his list, so in a carbon copy of my arrival in Egypt a year before, I was put on a lorry and sent to Abu Sueir.

Next morning, I ignored protocol and telephoned HQME in Cairo, where I eventually got hold of a staff officer who knew about 272 AMES. "That is going as far east as it can go: in fact, it's already gone, and I have made special arrangements for the ship to divert into Aden, to pick you up. What the hell are you doing in Egypt?"

After I had made some explanation, he said, "You'd better get back to Tewfik at once." So I checked out of the mess and caught a train back through Ismailia and down the canal to Port Tewfik again. I began to wish the RAF could make its mind up.

The only transit camp actually at Tewfik was a huge tented area, occupied almost entirely by the army and very crowded and primitive, but I found a corner of a tent in the officers' mess and was glad to use my camp kit for a night's rest after an evening meal, in a marquee lit by hurricane lamps.

The next day was a Sunday. I knew that HQME would be working and so I took a chance and accepted a lift from an army captain with a three-ton truck and whizzed up to Cairo. As I still had my HBM Forces in Egypt identity card (the "B" stood for "Britannic" so that we should not confuse George VI with Farouk). I was able to get into headquarters where I called on various staff officers I knew: they told me that I was booked on the first available ship for Colombo, so I had better be back in Tewfik "tomorrow at the latest".

No-one gave me a bed, so I got the last available room in the so-called "Grand" Hotel and passed a thoroughly miserable night. Grand was a bit of a euphemism, at least as far as my bedroom was concerned: it seemed to have been partitioned off out of a lift well, with an antiquated lift clanking and creaking up and down all night just by my ear. On the whole, even Tewfik transit camp was to be preferred and I left at dawn, hitching a lift across the desert to MEP at Kasfareit and then down the rest of the canal to Tewfik.

Fortunately I was in time, for I learned that I was due to sail in the morning and the poor adjutant had been trying to find me; it was a relief to find that someone actually knew I existed. That evening, March 9, another 100,000 Allied troops were surrendering to the Japanese in Java, and while the ship bearing 272 MRU with its whole complement of men and vehicles was calling into Aden just to embark me, I was watching an ENSA concert in Egypt.

On March 10, packed up once more, I spent many hours being processed from camp to quay, from quay to tender and from tender to ship, until I secured the extraordinary luxury of a single-berth cabin on the promenade deck of the P&O liner *Orontes*. I had been given a typed slip of paper authorising me to travel to Colombo, an RAF trooping draft of just one person, and I soon found out that I was indeed a unique specimen, for I was the only passenger who knew where I was going and the only Englishman among more than 2000 Australians.

This was a pretty tough set, for they were the remains of the very first Australian army who had gone to the Middle East and who had fought their way all through the Western Desert. Quite suddenly they had been withdrawn to Suez and put aboard the *Orontes*. To a man, they believed we were bound straight for Australia, and I felt it better to keep my counsel and not to tell even the officers with whom I shared my meal table where I was going and where I had good reason to believe they were going too.

These Aussies reminded me of great, overgrown Alsatian puppies—big, boisterous, cheerful and full of fun but liable to break anything in sight out of sheer exuberance. I talked with many of them including, often, the other ranks who were manning their own Bren guns on the boat deck

128

against possible air attack. One of these gave me a round of .303 tracer which I carried with my .455 ammo for the rest of the war, since I had heard that the quickest way to destroy radar vehicles and all their secrets was to put a tracer round through the petrol tank.

Another showed me, out of his pocket, a special round of .303 on which he had engraved a set of initials and which he was going to use to murder the initials' owner the next time they went into action. Something about his demeanour led me to believe him, for passions certainly ran high in this bunch of men.

Rumour had it that on their way out from Australia an unpopular RSM had, one day, been found to be no longer on board. I could believe that, too, after witnessing a casual incident on deck, when an NCO tried to break up an illicit card school and one of the diggers just casually eyed the NCO up and down and said, "Can you swim?" and then went back to his game. The NCO walked away, and so did I, feigning deafness.

None of these men had ever been to England, and when they had got used to my extraordinary accent I was able to tell them about the war in Europe and the London blitz, so different from shooting Italians in the desert which they had regarded in much the same light as shooting kangaroos in the bush back home.

Apart from me, this was entirely an army ship, and parades, training and medical inspections were going on all the time, mixed with PT and arms drill—anything to give the men something to do.

On one occasion this led to a tragedy. A couple of would-be commandos were practising an armed defence and taking it in turns to attack each other with a wicked-looking dagger with a handle incorporating a knuckleduster. The unarmed defender had to sidestep, grab the raised dagger arm and throw his assailant in one quick movement. All went well at first, but as the exercise was repeated at a faster and faster pace, quite random chance caused the dagger to lodge, point uppermost, between the two exercise mats and the man fell supine onto this dreadful spike, with a knife buried up to its hilt in his back.

I had some interesting mealtimes with the officers of this Australian force. One was an MP who had been at Cambridge University for a time and had joined up on the outbreak "to further my career as a politician". Another was the nephew of General Sir Thomas Blamey, GOC of all the Australian forces, and even he did not know we were not going straight back to Australia.

***

Four days out from Suez, on March 14, I saw looming up ahead the familiar outlines of Shum-shum and Aman Khal. I was back in Aden! The *Orontes* anchored in the outer harbour and for some reason, known perhaps to the Admiralty but certainly not to us, we stayed there for four days. No one was allowed ashore.

After two days I made special application to the OC Troops to go ashore and wind up my affairs and, as I was not a precedent for the Australians, I was allowed to go. The rail was lined with troops all saying things like "lucky Pommy bastard" as I joined the ship's purser for our run ashore and stepped once again onto "the barren rocks of Aden".

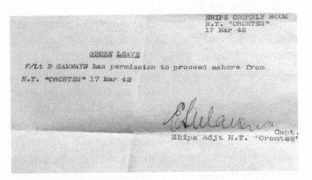

My first call on foot was to Barclays Bank (DC&O) where I had an account to close, full of all my unclaimed allowances. I drew the lot in cash, filling a pocket with a wad of notes, since in the likely trouble ahead I preferred to have my resources with me. Then, again on foot, I climbed all the way up to Aman Khal through the noonday heat to collect a few of my things that had been left behind and to have one more look at my last command.

There was naturally some surprise among the men at my reappearance and I shall never forget the look of horror on the face of one certain rather stupid young aircraftsman when I greeted him by name with a smile. I knew, and he knew I knew, that the last time we had looked into each other's eyes had been 16 days ago. I had stopped, several hundred feet down the mountain and turned for a last look, and he, peering over the wall at his departing CO, had been foolish enough to finger his nose.

"Hello …" I said (even today I could name him, but I won't), "I've come back." There was a long pause. Finally: "N-nice to s-see you Sir." I left it at that.

I made sure not to miss the launch back to the ship, but not before I had collected the batch of mail left behind on my last departure and sent a cable home. Early the next morning, the *Orontes* weighed anchor and I was up on deck to see the departure.

As we ploughed across the Indian Ocean, accompanied as escort by a grey-painted armed merchant cruiser (a number of smaller and faster liners had been hastily given some deck guns and anti-aircraft missiles and sailed under the white ensign) I followed the daily radio news carefully and learnt of the sweeping successes of the Japanese in the Pacific and how they now controlled the whole East Indies and were menacing Ceylon.

One evening, in particular, I heard a report of a member of the government in England, saying in parliament, "When the Japanese invade Ceylon, *as they surely will*, we shall defend the island to the last man." I remember particularly the use of when, and not if, and also the confidence with which he used the italicised words and I thought of how I had escaped the Crete affair and of the ease

131

with which the Japanese had taken Singapore and Hong Kong.

Now I was going (if I got there in time) to the very spot which was their next target. "As they surely will," the man had said, and who was I to disbelieve him?

So because I was scared, I did two things—I drank a double whisky (which helped a lot) and I began to work out a policy for personal survival in the event of capture. My first duty, should we be over-run by the enemy, was to safeguard the secrets of radar by destroying the equipment, together with the circuit diagrams and other secret documents, but what concerned me was the possibility of the Japanese trying to extract my technical knowledge as the officer commanding.

The chances of being able to take to the jungle, after waiting long enough to blow up or burn the equipment, were pretty slim, but it seemed sensible to see that two things, at least, were always about my person: my gun and my wad of money.

The only other strategy I could think of, and for which I made secret personal plans, was to cease to be an officer at the moment of capture by the simple expedience of slipping the two rings off the shoulder tabs of my khaki shirt (which was, in all other respects, identical with those worn by other ranks) and thus instantly transforming myself from 80926 Flight Lieutenant B Samways to 180926 A/C 2 Samways B.

Delighted that the six-figure number was plausible for a ranker while, should my capture ever get reported through the Red Cross, the Air Ministry might just possibly find the only Samways on their books was 80926 and work it out for themselves. Hopefully, then, my next of kin might be informed that I was "presumed POW" instead of "missing, presumed dead".

This improbable plan also involved getting any personnel to agree to say that our officer had deserted and left us to our fate, but of course this had to be left until the last moment, so I told no one of my ideas. Pathetic as this miserable plan sounds, it was the best I could devise and shows that I was at least trying to think ahead—which was more than could be said for those who had planned to defend Singapore with fixed guns that could not be brought to bear on the attacking Japanese.

In contrast to these rather gloomy forebodings for the immediate future, the present, in the shape of a first class, luxury sun cruise across the Indian Ocean, was very pleasant. I much enjoyed the company of the Australian officers and joined in with them for a formal mess dinner, for which I dug out my best "blue" to dine in style, while the regimental band played "Sussex by the Sea" (especially for me, poor Pommy) together with their own home tunes.

***

Seven days out from Aden, we made a landfall at dawn off Colombo, and we all gazed at the long, low, green line of palm trees overtopped by the hideous sky sign erected behind the harbour which advertised Ceylon Tea. Although we moored up in the harbour by 10 am, it was not until next day, Thursday March 26, that anyone disembarked. I got ashore with the first batch of junior officers, said goodbye to my Australian friends and tried to find out what I was supposed to do.

Eventually I found a temporary office, staffed by a girl secretary, who said that surplus officers in transit had to go to the Galle Face Hotel and wait for orders. So there I went. The Galle Face, splendidly situated at the end of the Galle Face Green, was the premier, colonial style luxury hotel of the island and it was full of planters' wives and children all waiting for shipping to evacuate them to South Africa. The only accommodation for me was six feet of floor space on the floor of the ballroom, and here I put up my camp bed along with numbers of other officers from the services, all huddled together.

By word of mouth I learned that the senior radio officer (we still used euphemisms to disguise the real nature of our work) was Squadron Leader Floyd and that he had a room in the hotel. Now William Floyd had been a pilot officer on the same course as me at Yatesbury, and now here he was a senior officer and my boss, but where was he? The best I could do was to extract his room number from the reception—but he was out, so I was reduced to leaving a note in his pigeonhole and waiting.

I waited all day, getting more and more frustrated, until in the evening I went off with some new-found friends to the racecourse which had been hastily and successfully knocked into a possible airstrip by requisitioning the old Ladies Golf Course alongside. In a very short time this was to prove of great value and its secrecy was the only saving grace for the RAF.

Here, in a requisitioned house behind the grandstand, I spent a convivial evening with a few other RDF officers, including H.G. David from Bristol and Al Roberts from Canada. They were not a bit surprised that I hadn't yet found Floyd, but they said he was dashing around requisitioning things in all directions and generally showing a lot of dynamism, which I found rather encouraging after the torpor of Aden. I took a rickshaw back to the Galle Face to find my note still in Floyd's pigeonhole and settled down to wait.

Nothing happened all next morning (didn't he even come in to eat or sleep?) until suddenly, long past lunchtime, in strode Willie, all very autocratic and self-important (it seemed to me) in his elevated rank of squadron leader.

"Ah, Samways," he said (what's the matter with Bruce? I thought; we are supposed to know each other but let it pass). "Samways. My staff car is at the door. You are to go in it at once to Ratmalana where a plane will take you to Trincomalee," and he turned to go.

"What about my kit?" I asked.

"I'll send it on. You'd better hurry," and he was gone. Well, here was action and gladly I ran to the car and was driven off at high speed down through the crowded streets and the ramshackle boutiques that lined them on the

134

southern road towards Galle. A few miles out of Colombo was the prewar civil aerodrome of Ratmalana, now under the command of the RAF. It was a grass aerodrome, rather like a circular cricket pitch surrounded by palm trees, with a couple of hangars and an apology for a control tower.

I ran to the tower and shouted up to a man on the balcony, "Have you got an aircraft going to Trinco?"

"That's it, taking off now. I'll stop it for you if you like." With that he picked up a Very pistol and fired a red flare, and as this soared into the sky I saw that it was meant to halt a Swordfish which was already trundling across the grass for takeoff. The Stringbag slowed and stopped, then taxied back to us.

"I've got to go to Trinco," I said.

"Hop in," said the pilot, and with no introduction or other formality I climbed up into the observer's cockpit behind him and we were off. It is no exaggeration to say that this was a pretty important flight to catch and although of course this is only speculation, it is just possible that if I had missed my connection we might just possibly have lost the whole war.

One cannot write of the Swordfish aircraft without nostalgia. These open-cockpit, be-wired and be-strutted biplanes, which could take off in 50 yards, were to me "real" aeroplanes. To fly in one was to have the wind in your hair, to enjoy flying like a bird does, unrestrained by metal and Perspex from contact with the elements and with the ground or the sea slipping past you only a few feet below. Exhilarating!

This particular aeroplane in which I now flew northeast across the island was to be shot down by the Japanese just nine days later.

For the present, I was enjoying the spectacular views as we flew across the mountainous interior, the palm trees giving way to rubber and the rubber plantations giving way to tea. Then we dropped down again to the flatter jungle areas of the northeast, with their fantastic prehistoric "tanks", huge irrigation lakes contained by earth-wall dams,

135

the products of slave labour in the earlier Kandyan kingdoms.

At Kantalai tank my pilot indicated that he was going to do a simulated torpedo attack and we skimmed over the water at a height of a few feet (I remember looking UP at the branches of the trees which were overhanging the long straight bund containing the water) and then, at the last moment, he slipped the Swordfish up and over the rock he had chosen for the role of a Japanese battleship. It was just the sheer joy of flying.

Flying to Trincomalee in the ill-fated Swordfish
– over Kantalai tank

Soon there came into view the east coast, with the splendid natural harbour of Trincomalee, and beside it the aerodrome known as China Bay, where we touched down. I was met by Squadron Leader Carter. He was glad to see me because now I had come, he could get back to India. It seemed that Floyd had asked him to keep an eye on the assembly of 272 MRU at China Bay, and its eventual removal to a site at Elizabeth Point, a few miles to the north, where he would take me.

With no further introduction, I climbed into a little Morris 8, which Carter seemed to have, and was driven off around the northern shores of the harbour into Trincomalee town and then up the northern coast road into the jungle. Of troops or defences, I saw no sign, even at what was apparently the only possible natural line of resistance, where the road crossed a salty tidal marshy area (which would no doubt be flooded in the wet monsoon) over a series of bridges and culverts.

Past these, returning seawards down a dirt road through mixed palm trees and jungle scrub for a couple of miles, we reached what seem to be a deserted farm field of perhaps two acres, bordering on the beach to the east and bounded by a group of coconut palms to the south and by more jungle to the north. This was my site, and its only amenity was a well full of rather depressing-looking greenish slimy water.

I stood on the edge of the beach and looked pensively out to sea. In any normal times this would have been perfect for a holiday—a truly tropical island shoreline, palm-fringed and bathed in hot sunlight; but all that lay between me and the horizon (over which I could already, in my imagination, see a fleet of Japanese warships steaming in) was a strip of sand— not so much as a single strand of barbed wire and no army within miles—if we had an army at all.

When the Japanese landed to take Trincomalee, this, the first open beach to the north of the harbour, was sure to be their landing place. I said to Carter, "What do you think would happen if I refused to bring my unit here but put it up somewhere in the harbour area?"

He was not very helpful. "You'd either get a medal or a court-martial," he said. "Come on, let's get back to the hotel. It's all yours now," with which, still thoughtful, I turned my back on the sea and we drove back up the track to the road over the swamp and down a few miles of road to Trincomalee.

On a little rocky promontory, one of many projecting into the harbour, stood the Welcombe Hotel which still bore some of the marks of civilisation and which was still operating as a hotel, although it was only days away from being requisitioned by the military. Here I got a meal and a bed for the night, all the while seething with suppressed anger at the apparent lack of preparation of any sort of credible defence against attack on this, the finest deep-water harbour in the whole Indian Ocean.

Over breakfast the next morning (the last civilised meal I was to have for many weeks) I listened, without comment, to my senior officer's plans for the installation of my station. He had, he said, made arrangements for Works and Buildings to make two concrete foundations for the two masts. (Big deal! Aren't we supposed to be a mobile unit? Let it pass!)

Meanwhile the airmen were all in barracks at China Bay while my adjutant, Flying Officer Nielsen, was in the officers' mess there. (Not for long he isn't, I thought.) A forward party was supposed to be preparing an "admin and sleeping" site a couple of miles up the coast because the technical site was malarial ...

On he went, outlining a programme which would take weeks to complete, and I began to wonder whether the Japs would wait that long. I certainly would not.

Chapter 10

Elizabeth Point

Happily, I found that the little Morris car was, in fact, part of my own unit transport, so I used it to drive my squadron leader to China Bay Officers' Mess. I never saw him again.

From that same mess I soon extracted my adjutant, Flying Officer Nielsen, and one glance was enough to explain why he was nicknamed "Poonah". This upright, ramrod of a man had all the bearing of a cavalry officer and all the mannerisms of the typical English gentleman in India, for he had spent 25 years in the Indian police, mostly, I understood, playing polo and suppressing riots. He wore a monocle with all the accustomed ease with which other people wear hats, and I knew he would be a valuable ally, knowing the local rules and understanding discipline.

'Poonah' in the native market

No more than twice my age, he took my orders without hesitation, the first order being that my whole unit was to move out of China Bay at once, with a technical convoy going to the site, and the remaining transport and personnel to go to the admin location. He was to be responsible for saying that the two camps were established and fed and watered before dark.

I had never before even seen a complete mobile radio unit, let alone trained and drilled a crew in its operation, and I soon found that none of my men was any more experienced than I was, for we had all been thrown together out of the Middle East melting pot, leftovers from other parts of the radar system, and mostly raw out of England—but at least it was a complete self-contained outfit on paper.

The transmitter and receiver were each housed in a purpose-built three-ton Thornycroft lorry, and each held a flatbed trailer which bore its own 105-foot tower, broken down into six sections for transport. Three other three-tonners carried all the tentage and equipment for a crew of over 55 men, and each pulled its own trailer; there were two 15 kW diesel-electric generators and a water bowser.

Besides the radio mechanics and radio operators I had a full complement of drivers–MT, cooks and butchers, corporals SP (all service police had the rank of acting corporal, and I had four of them to provide 24-hour guard duty), a medical orderly and even some ACH G-Ds {which meant aircraft hands, general duties).

As this impressive looking convoy was getting ready to leave China Bay, one of my sergeants staggered up with a huge sack over his shoulder, just like Father Christmas, but instead of toys it was full of tins of bully beef. These he had scrounged from a fellow sergeant cook in the camp, with the thought that we ought to have some iron rations as we set off into the blue under an unknown and inexperienced commanding officer. This was a wise precaution, as we shall see.

The only concession to our comfort for those first few days was a single PIP tent. This European Personnel, Indian Pattern tent would just hold four camp beds, and this became home to Nielsen and me and Sergeants Lee and Shuttleworth, all sharing together.

Lee was a regular, a wireless operator by trade and, I think, the only regular airman in the whole crew; his responsibility was communications. Bob Shuttleworth, a volunteer, had been a wireless serviceman before the war. He had a quiet, relaxed, even lazy-looking manner but was a tower of strength and, like me, he was very keen to get things moving. I soon found that he was able to get things done on his own initiative, starting with the diesel generators which he coaxed into life to provide power.

The C.O. and F/Sgt Shuttleworth outside the PIP tent

With no organisation at all (I did not have even a nominal roll of the men in my command) everyone seemed to take to his trade task with a will. The medical orderly condemned the well on the site but found another nearby for our water supply, the Cs and Bs fell to cooking and butchering to feed us, the SPs set up a guard, the ACHs dug latrines while the R-Ops and R-Mechs set about the mast assembly and the W-Ops tried in vain to make WT contact with Colombo.

The rest of the personnel were supposed to be setting up our "domestic" camp in the malaria-free zone up the coast, but as the sunset approached I became increasingly worried at the thought of having my troops split into two locations. All we had with which to defend ourselves against the Japanese Imperial Navy were six Lee Enfield rifles and one box of ammunition, and I needed all the support possible to avoid capture long enough to enable me to destroy our secret equipment.

So I sent one of the acting corporal SPs off to the domestic camp with an instruction that all personnel there were to strike tents and come at once to the technical site.

Half an hour later the man was back, but alone. "They won't come," he said, "because they say they are supposed to stay there."

"But you are an NCO and I gave you an order," I exploded. The man hung his head and I could see that he was still a misplaced shop assistant at heart, with no sense at all of the urgency of the situation we were in or of his duty to follow his orders unto death—indeed unto a death which I could see already as a possibility for all of us before the night was over.

The corporal would have to wait, for much more serious than his weakness was the mutiny of the men who had refused to leave their supposedly malaria-free sanctuary. Mutiny is a strong word, but that is what I was faced with, a collective disobedience—not only on active service but, for all I knew, in imminent danger of an enemy attack. My band of mutineers had to be brought to heel at once.

"Sergeant Shuttleworth," I said, "take the corporal's revolver off him, go to the other camp and bring all the men here at once. Put them on parade here—and if any man disobeys you can shoot him."

This was neither bravado nor bluff on my part; goodness knows what would've happened if he had actually shot one of the men, and I never stopped to think.

Fortunately, perhaps, this strong and unequivocal lead was all that was needed, and as tropical day gave way to tropical night the lorries rumbled into camp and the splendid Shuttleworth paraded all hands in the little clearing under the light of a string of naked light bulbs powered from our throbbing diesel generator. (I had already decided to ignore the official blackout and to work day and night alike until we were on the air.)

I walked up and down in front of the ranks of now rather sheepish-looking airmen and, without distinguishing in any way the mutineers from the innocent, gave the whole lot a verbal blasting in forthright terms. I made it clear, beyond any doubt, that I was too busy to bother with formal discipline and would have no more disobedience of any sort at any time; that we might all just possibly save our own miserable skins, when the Japanese landed, if we kept together as a unit—but not if they were spread all over the … island. And now they could get back to work and God help them if they disobeyed my orders again.

This rough justice was taken in good part by almost all of the men, who seemed happy enough now they knew who was boss, and it soon came back to me that there had been a ringleader of sorts, an MT driver who had tried to convince them that the MO took precedence and they were safe to ignore me. Next day, giving no reason, I sent him off to China Bay and with the connivance of the Station Warrant Officer had him posted.

***

We all fell to work on the assembly and erection of the two towers; it was like giving a set of grown-up children an enormous Meccano set but no instruction book, and none of us had ever put one up before.

But the design was very clever and deserves a description. They were made almost entirely of wood, bolted together with fishplates and galvanised nuts and bolts so that they were non-conductive. The cross-section was a square,

143

starting with a square steel base 4 feet by 4 feet, from which the uprights diverged to the 35-foot level, where the square was 5 feet by 5 feet, and then tapered into a 1 foot by 1 foot square at the maximum height of 105 feet. The main timbers, some 2 inches square at the base, got thinner and thinner towards the top, the uppermost being no more than 1 inch square.

Our first task was to lay out all the frameworks along the ground, bolting them together into one rigid, prostrate structure, with a pair of legs on the base frame forming hinges with a pair of short axles on the base plate. It was obvious that we were meant to haul the tower up by winch about this hinge until two lugs on the other two corners engaged their sockets. But (and here was the beauty of the design) these lugs were only guides, allowing considerable play and movement, while the whole weight of the tower would sit on a single ball and socket in the centre of the base plate, able to sway and bend in the wind and kept upright only by the diagonal guys.

There were two sets of guy wires, from the 35-foot and 87-foot levels, each pair coming down to a single steel picket, set accurately on the diagonal at just the right distance away. I stood back and surveyed the first recumbent giant (looking for all the world like a prone Gulliver, swarming with Lilliputians) and knew that I soon had to take the responsibility for hauling it upright. It was a daunting thought that if anything went wrong I should be left with a crumpled mass of firewood and, worse, that Trincomalee would have no early warning; so I checked and rechecked the tightness of the bolts and the length and security of the guys until all seemed sound.

We positioned the winch lorry accurately on the centreline, down on the beach due east, and ran out the cable which would lead up and over the top of a boom and then shackled to the pair of main guys on the upmost face of the recumbent tower.

As the cable took the strain, the timber of the tower quivered and creaked and seemed to come alive as,

144

agonisingly slowly, the whole framework inched upwards. At an angle of about 15 degrees the cable rose from the notch on the end of the boom and took the whole dead weight.

'The recumbent giant' - The first tower before erection – note the sag under its own weight

This was obviously the moment of greatest strain, when any give on the winch lorry or the tower base could be disastrous. So we hurried on with the winching until, sweet as a nut, the forward lugs engaged with the notches on the baseplate corners and the whole weight stood on the ball and socket joint. Anxious hands secured the secondary guys and it was then safe to adjust the main guys and shackle them home.

No angler, landing his first salmon, could have been prouder than I was at the successful raising. For a trained and experienced crew it would have been nothing remarkable, but to us it was like making the first solo flight without having any flying lessons—no room for error and only one chance to get it right!

With the receiver mast safely upright, work could go ahead with installing the aerials and feeder system, and the next task was to get the transmitter mast up.

Alas, when this was nearly assembled, we found several vital pieces missing, including a pair of diagonal steel braces and two of the four main steel guys. The originals must have been left in Egypt (or possibly had never left England), so I had to take a chance on local improvisation.

The steel braces I replaced with improvised timber struts—they looked to be strong enough and anyway there was no choice—but for the steel cables I could only use ordinary hemp rope which I extracted from the stores at China Bay. This again looked strong enough but was obviously too stretchy and would need constant watching with changes in the humidity, if I could not replace them before the monsoon broke.

The transmitter aerial array was much more cumbersome than the receiver array, so it was mostly assembled onto the mast face before erection and then, fingers crossed, we took the first strain on the lifting cable and then re-inspected our jury-rigged wooden braces under load, before pulling away and up and trusting the whole future of our enterprise to two strips of packing case deputising for half-inch steel plates.

It was now Monday March 30. In no more than 48 hours on site we had our masts up, our diesels running, our T&R vans in position, and all was ready for wiring up. I was desperately keen to get on the air as quickly as possible, and by working again through the night I hoped to be operational before dawn.

From the top of the tower

But there was a snag. Our supposedly direct means of communication with the fighter control room at China Bay was by wireless telegraphy, and for some reason our W/Ops failed to open up a satisfactory link. I was also supposed to operate a security system which meant coding every grid reference into a different false reference (with a code which was constantly changing), sending this by Morse code and then having the signal decoded and plotted.

It all seemed a crazy waste of time, even if we had had a working, two-way link, so I decided that only a telephone line would do, and a line I must have. I jumped into the little Morris 8 and drove as fast as I could to China Bay. In my innocence I thought that everyone knew by now that we were at war, with only precious moments left to us to prepare to try to beat off a Japanese attack. This simple faith was about to take me into the most bizarre experience of my whole career, and it happened like this.

I stopped outside SHQ and walked down the row of offices, all with doors and windows wide open, until I came to one marked "Commanding Officer". I just walked straight in, saluted, and said, "Please sir, I want a telephone line at once."

The group captain looked me up and down." Why aren't you shaved?" he said. I replied something to the effect that I hadn't had time. "Then you should get up earlier in the morning."

For a moment I was lost for words. To say the truth—that I could not have got up earlier because I hadn't been to bed all night, but anyway my razor and all my kit was still in Colombo and didn't he know there was a war on?—would not have been exactly discreet, so I just stared at him goggle-eyed, dirty and sweaty as I was. He pressed the bell push on his desk and the station adjutant immediately came in from the next office.

"Take this 'officer'," he said (and I could hear the inverted commas, heavy with sarcasm, in his tone) -"take this 'officer' to the mess. He is to have a bath and a shave and then report back to me."

With that, he dropped his eyes to the file on his desk and the interview was over. I followed the adjutant out of the office and then, leaving the poor man standing, just walked off. It was, I suppose, a court-martial offence to disobey an order from a superior officer, but I never gave it a second thought, and if the group captain wouldn't give me a telephone I'd have to find someone who would.

Further down the block I came to an office bearing the sign "Station Signals Officer" so I just marched in, saluted and found myself talking to Squadron Leader (as he was then) Robert Louis. Here was another regular serving officer, but how different! An avuncular figure of some 40 years of age, he listened to my story in silence and then said

148

simply, "Okay son, just you go back to your station and get it on the air. I'll have you a telephone line in before dawn."

He did just that, to me a minor miracle, and this is how. Some four miles from my site, over jungle tracks, was a pre-World War I naval gallery observation post, stone-built onto a rock sticking up through the jungle trees. There was presumably a similar one 10 miles down the coast, so that cross bearings could be taken on any Dutch or Portuguese man-of-war which dared to come within range of Trincomalee shore-based batteries on Fort Frederick.

This OP was linked through to Naval HQ and so to China Bay, and was in effect my nearest telephone. Working through the night, Squadron Leader Louis had a team of signallers lay a field telephone line, reel after reel of it, until the gap was closed, and so proudly I was able to report "272 MRU on the air" over my own tie-line, at 09.00 hours on March 31.

I suppose this news must have been reported to the station commander at China Bay, but I heard nothing from him, either by way of congratulation or court-martial—not then, or ever. (In fact, ten days later he was posted out of the island.)

However, on April 1, the official birthday of the Royal Air Force, I received a telegram of congratulations from the AOC himself, Air Vice Marshal D'Albiac, who acknowledged, "This must have entailed a great deal of hard work."

This little gesture from the great man was much appreciated, especially as he must have had much to occupy his mind, but on his shoulders lay all the burden of the defence of the island. The day before, as I came on the air, the Eastern Fleet of the Royal Navy had left the island to avoid its inevitable destruction by the Japanese fleet which, intelligence reported, would strike at Ceylon on April 1 or 2.

The Japanese had, available aboard their five carriers, about 15 attack aircraft for every one of our defensive fighters, and so the RN took the path of discretion and left the RAF to provide the valour.

As in the Battle of Britain, such an enormous disadvantage in numbers would have been decisive without the early warning and fighter direction facilities which radar provided. Bob Louis, at least, understood this, and he became a frequent visitor and provider—not only of field telephone lines but also of information and test flights and anything else he could do to help. He also liked to come for the swimming, for it was now possible, with the massive effort of installation over, to spend the hottest part of the day in the water—of which more later.

***

In fact, apart from the war, and the mosquitoes and malaria and the snakes, our situation was nothing short of idyllic, with all of the attributes of the mythical South Sea Island— golden sand, swaying palms, clear blue sea, moonlit nights. That April 1 was, in fact, the night of a full moon, and I can still recall how the front of the coconut palms glistened in the moonlight and the track of the moon's reflection lay over the sea to the east.

But the full moon, as we well knew from the Battle of Britain, was a time of danger, when an attacking force would have the advantage whether he came by air or by sea. As well as a non-stop radar watch on the skies, I posted sentries through the night, while those off duty could now snatch some sleep. Thus it was, in that "darkest hour before the dawn", that I was shaken out of my sleep by an anxious young man who had seen a light winking out at sea.

I hardly expected a full-scale invasion with no notice (surely the navy must be somewhere in the Indian Ocean), but we had heard stories of parachutists landing in Kandy and infiltration from the submarine might well be coming ashore for spying or sabotage. Feeling anything but brave, and pistol in hand, I walked down the beach with the lad and, sure enough, there was a twinkling light just above the eastern horizon.

We watched and waited. And then I saw another, fainter and even closer to the water, then a third; and then slowly the truth forced its way into my sleep-befuddled brain. With the moon already down behind the inland mountains and the sun not yet risen, we were watching the star-rise. I thought of the lines from Ulysses: "… and sail beyond / the baths of all the western stars / until we die".

But of course, Ulysses was going west, and we were looking east, so our stars were coming up, not down. It seemed as though we were going to live through another dawn.

The first four days of April passed without an enemy attack—days we spent in active cooperation with the Fleet Air Arm Swordfish squadrons who flew test flights at my request to check the range of our cover at different heights, and in a crude attempt at calibrating our receiver system for height finding. Back in England, height finding calibration on the chain stations was a specialised business carried out by a senior visiting officer from Group HQ, but here in the jungle it was up to me to do my best on my own resources and on my memory from the Yatesbury theory lessons, allied to my physics and mathematics background from Cambridge.

The theory was relatively simple: an aircraft received a pulse of radiation from our transmitter in two ways: first the direct line path through the air and secondly the reflected pulse off the surface of the sea.

This reflected pulse could be thought of as coming from an imaginary aerial as far below ground level as the actual aerial was above ground (rather like looking at a street lamp and also its reflection in a puddle). The reflected ray, due to its reflection, was exactly half a wavelength different in phase from the direct ray. So exactly along the surface there was no net signal since the direct and reflected rays exactly cancelled each other out, but at a certain small angle up from the horizontal, the reflected ray, having gone down to the surface and bounced up again, had travelled an extra distance to make up the half wavelength, and so the two signals reinforced, and the aircraft was "illuminated".

From the known aerial height and known wavelength, one could calculate the angle of the lowest "beam" or "lobe" (at which any aircraft would give the strongest return signal) and also the next "extinction" angle (when an incoming signal would fade) before the secondary lobe and so on. In the main, it was the lowest lobe which covered most of the operation, especially for targets several miles away, and so the knowledge of the signal strength and lobe angle, allied to the range, would give a very crude idea of the height, no more.

In an effort to make a better measurement, the theory was to use a secondary receiver at a lower height, whose lobe would be shorter, fatter and at a higher angle than the main lobe. If one then compared the two signal strengths from the two aerials, one could in theory determine the true, very small, angle above the horizon of the incoming signal and hence the height.

All of this of course depended on the reflecting surface; and this was most of the sea. I already knew that this rose and fell with the tide, effectively changing the aerial height all the time. Despite all these problems, I did achieve some sort of calibration for height finding during those first four days of operation.

Easter Sunday, April 5, 1942, brought the anticipated attack on the island. It was, from the Japanese point of view, a carbon copy of Pearl Harbor, achieving total tactical surprise over the Allied forces on a sleepy Sunday morning, in the shape of a mass air raid on Colombo Harbour.

It is said that at Pearl Harbor the incoming Japanese aircraft were seen by American radar but were either ignored or falsely identified as friendly, so that no early warning was given. It seems unbelievable that the same thing could happen at Colombo, where 254 MRU was supposed to be in operation on a site on the golf course.

Even now it is not up to me to say what went wrong, but in fact (and for whatever reason) the radar system failed to give any warning and astonished squadron commanders found themselves looking up at Japanese aircraft filling the sky while their own Hurricanes were still on the ground. Air Vice Marshal D'Albiac is quoted as saying, "I shall never get over this."

However, from the RAF point of view, all was not lost—not quite. A brilliant piece of adaptive work, carried out very quickly and ruthlessly, had converted the Colombo racecourse and the adjoining ladies' golf course into an airstrip where the Hurricanes and Blenheims were based, with the planes concealed under the spreading trees which lined the adjoining city avenues. This was unknown to the Japanese, who directed their attacks on the old civil airport at Ratmalana and on the harbour, and consequently the RAF was able to get its fighters belatedly airborne instead of having them all destroyed on the ground.

The Fleet Air Arm was less fortunate, and by chance their squadron of Swordfish arrived in the Colombo airspace (having flown down from China Bay) at the height of the battle. They were all lost.

To the Japanese, the attack must have seemed to be both a success and a failure—successful in that as at Pearl Harbor they had been able to fly in, in mass formations, and arrive at their target unopposed; but a failure because the big units of the British fleet had slipped away and they were denied their main objective.

However, they sank both naval and merchant shipping in Colombo Harbour with only minimal losses, only two Japanese aircrew being shot down over land. These two crashed at Mount Lavinia and they were buried in the grounds of the services hospital there.

The news of the attack on Colombo reached us on our side of the island as soon as the raid started, and naturally we had no way of knowing that a simultaneous attack on us was not imminent. If we needed any spur to keep us on the alert, the knowledge that somehow the

153

Colombo station had failed to give proper warning redoubled our efforts, and I kept a personal check on the little cathode ray tube throughout the day.

But the only activity to the east all day were our own aircraft flying reconnaissance patrols, usually the so-called crossover patrol, in which they swept two paths, each across the line of advance of the enemy but spaced apart so that the maximum rectangle of sea was covered.

We passed that Easter Day, therefore, in a state of continuous apprehension and alert against an air attack, and as darkness fell with the usual tropical suddenness we had not only to maintain our watch over the skies but also consider a seaborne raid on our defenceless beach. I felt entitled to some sleep myself, so I deputised Nielsen to mount and command an all-night guard from the non-radar personnel (using our six pathetic rifles) and, as he had no weapon of his own, I decided to give him my Colt .455 for his tour of duty.

As it happened, we were discussing these arrangements as we sat side-by-side on my camp bed in the single tent which housed Nielsen and me and our two senior NCOs. The only lighting was a hurricane lamp hanging down from the ridge pole, shining down on our four pairs of legs and feet in the narrow space between the camp beds.

I handed over the heavy automatic and the clip of cartridges after demonstrating how it was to be loaded, and then, just as I was choosing a password for the night, BANG! there was an almighty explosion just by my left ear. Poor Nielsen, used to revolvers all his life, had somehow managed to discharge the gun. Of course he had instinctively pointed it down to the ground, but as luck would have it, the proximity of the tent pole had meant that his feet were not wide enough apart and the blunt nosed .455 round went straight through his foot.

We cut off his shoe and sock and I used my first field dressing to hold the remains of his foot together while Sergeant Lee ran off to fetch the medical orderly. This lad (who should have known better) took off my dressing and replaced it with an identical one, but I suppose he thought he ought to show off his medical knowledge.

We carried the casualty to the little Morris car, and leaving Shuttleworth in charge, I drove the patient off towards Trincomalee and the naval hospital, only to be stopped by an armed sentry as soon as we reached the main road bridge over the creek. I found myself looking down the barrel of a rifle, held by a turbaned Indian soldier who could speak no English. Nielsen swore at him in Urdu, but he just stood there. I swore to him in English, with even less effect.

To break the impasse, I just pushed his rifle aside and drove off, only to be stopped again in a quarter of a mile, this time by a group of Indians and an NCO, who had enough English to explain that his orders were to let no one pass, and who refused to open his roadblock. I demanded to see his officer-sahib, and with Nielsen left bleeding in my car, I had to pick my way off into the jungle with a rifle pointed at the small of my back until we came to a concealed, tented, detachment of troops, all Indians, under an Indian officer. This latter was reclining on a camp bed and showed no sign of moving, so I lost my temper and shouted, "What's your rank?"

"Second lieutenant."

"Then stand up when you speak to me."

He was probably anxious not to lose face in front of his IOR, but slowly and languidly he climbed to his feet and asked to see my pass, explaining that I had no business to be outside his defence line, because he was the farthest outpost. He knew nothing of any RAF station and anyway his orders were that we were to be invaded by the Japanese before dawn.

Somehow I got him to understand that I was not only going to Trincomalee but I was also coming back again later. "Well," he said, "you can go, but you must drive without lights," (a proviso which I ignored as soon as I was out of range) and we saw no further troops all the way into Trinco.

I left Poonah in the hospital and turned out of the dockyard gates. Such information as I had been able to glean within the naval base tended to confirm the idea that the invasion was indeed expected before dawn, and just for a moment the thought of staying within the base was a temptation, instead of going back to the beach to be shot or bayoneted by a Japanese. It was only a passing thought, and no doubt enough for any serviceman who suddenly found himself alone and unobserved, able to run away and hide with no-one to see. It is much easier to be brave in company, so I hurried back to my men and my command.

***

The attack on Colombo left no-one in doubt that our turn to be the target would be next on the list, and suddenly my little station became of great interest to the fortress commander of Trincomalee, Admiral Palliser, who arrived unexpectedly to see for himself and demanded to see the commanding officer at once. With his flag lieutenant dutifully three paces in the rear, he marched down the sands at the direction of the corporal SP and waited for me to emerge from the waves, for I was taking a much-needed bath.

It is really quite unnerving to have to stand to attention, ankle-deep in the Indian Ocean and stark naked under the quarterdeck stare of a full admiral. I could not even salute, having no hat on, so I made what excuse I could and fled to my tent, where I donned my one dirty shirt and only pair of shorts (still wet) and reported back at the double, in the time it took the admiral to walk from the water's edge to the gallery where I showed him over the operation.

His visit brought quick results—within hours a small detachment of the Ceylon Garrison Artillery arrived to give us some protection, although they could do little but dig slit trenches from which to poke their rifles. I gave them strict orders that they were not to fire unless attacked first, as I felt it better that we should, if possible, not draw attention to

156

ourselves and just keep operating in the hope that the enemy would not know we were there.

I received another visitor that day, from the RAF MO from China Bay who was on his way up the coast to a secret airstrip at Kokkila, where some of the Hurricanes were at dispersal. He left me a written instruction that all personnel were to sleep under mosquito nets—and that, sadly, was the last order he ever gave. Two hours later he died when the aircraft in which he hoped to fly back to China Bay crashed on take-off.

All through these anxious days, and indeed ever since I left Aden, I had had no word of any sort from home. Nevertheless, I managed to keep to my self-imposed rule of writing at least a few lines to Peggy each and every day, and these composite letters would be posted every few days to take anything up to 12 weeks to travel round the Cape to England. It was a tenuous contact, but we both clung to it tenaciously.

The three days following the Colombo raid were used by the Japanese flotilla in a relentless pursuit of the Allied ships which had been dispersed, convoy-less, from Colombo when the British fleet put to sea. News came to us of many sinkings in the Bay of Bengal and stories too of Japanese submarines shelling open boats—and even taking survivors on board the casing, so that they could take any women below before closing the hatch and submerging, leaving the men to drown.

True or false? We had no way of knowing, for rumour is rife in wartime, but we had among us a few men who had escaped from Malaya and who knew how totally ruthless the Japanese could be, and we had no hope that, if captured, we would get Geneva Convention treatment.

Chapter 11

The raid of Trincomalee

Every morning I was called before sunrise so that I could personally be certain that we did not fail, and on the morning of April 9, four days after the Colombo attack, we saw an echo at the unbelievable range of 92 miles. The normal maximum operational arrange for an MRU with 105-foot masts was 60 to 70 miles for a very high-flying aircraft, so I knew that we either had a spurious echo—or else this was it!

It needed only a few seconds' observation of the way the signal bounced in the long grass of the time base, and of the width of the blip, to convince me that here was a lot of aircraft and not a single reconnaissance plane at an enormous height. I gave a provisional estimate of 10-plus at Angels 15, range 92, bearing 090 degrees, and we started the plot, passing the grid references direct to China Bay over our precious land line and thus giving them only a little under 100 miles of early warning.

I can only imagine the scene in the hastily contrived ops room at China Bay, where Walter Long, a filter officer newly arrived from Colombo, was doing his best. As we were the only station, he had no other reference to cross-check our information against, but he immediately reclassified our X-raid into a Hostile, and the squadrons went into action. It was soon apparent that the range was closing rapidly, which meant that the formation was on its way in and not just forming up over the carriers.

Very soon we detected further echoes following the first "hostile" in from the same bearing, and before long I was given an estimate of 10-plus on each of four blips, now nearly saturating the receiver and merging to make an ugly gap 15 miles long in the time-base. With such a confused echo beating up and down as the responses from individual aircraft beat in and out of phase, accurate height finding was impossible, but I thought it right to raise my estimate to Angels18.

At range 40 and closing for the leading edge of the blip, I went outside and looked at the beauty of the morning. It was an uncanny feeling to see such utter peace and silence, brilliant sun and clear blue sky, sparkling sea and golden sand—and to know beyond all doubt that death and destruction were coming straight at us at some 200 mph. Maybe we had only 12, no, 10 minutes left to enjoy life.

I passed word to the guard and to all off-duty airmen to take to the slit trenches and then just stood and listened. I could hear the ranges and bearings called from the R wagon and the constant bearing told me that we were indeed directly under the flight path. At eight miles (when the leading edge of the echo was already nearly lost in the ground wave—the direct signal from T to R that swamped the beginning of the time-base), I could hear the hum of engines, like a distant swarm of bees and I passed word into the receiver to give an "audible". However, stare as hard as I might, I could see nothing against the strength of the climbing sun, a factor which doubtless the Japanese had taken into account in the timing and direction of their attack.

And then, overhead and to the south across the mouth of Trincomalee Harbour, I could see wave after wave of silvery glistening dots, in perfect formation. Through the binoculars (the same Ross 8 x 40 which the vicar of Gillingham had loaned to me for the duration) I could make out, I felt sure, that there were twin-engine bombers among them, and I passed this information too on to China Bay. (It was disbelieved, and I was told I was probably seeing fighters with overload tanks. In fact, I was right, which shows how scant was the knowledge we possessed of the enemy.)

Happily, China Bay had believed our radar plots and the numbers of aircraft I had estimated, so nothing was kept in reserve. All 15 serviceable Hurricanes were sent up, a three and a six from China Bay with another flight of six taking off from the dispersal at Kokkilai. Even the six FAA Fulmars, no match for a modern fighter, took off as well; it may well have been thought that they were safer aloft than on the ground, with good reason, but they joined in the attack as best they could.

The Japanese bombers were able to maintain their formation almost unscathed through to their targets, because the fighter screen outnumbered our attacking Hurricanes by some five to one. But the very fact that they were intercepted at all on their run in was immediately reported to Admiral Nagumo and although we were never to know the extent of the Japanese losses, they must have been greater than in Colombo.

Added to that, they saw no aircraft on the ground at China Bay, a tribute to our early warning. Neither did they find any capital ships in Trincomalee Harbour, only the old monitor *Erebus*. Even the carrier *Hermes* had gone, but what shipping they did find they sank with ease. The attack on China Bay was severe, as we soon learned over our direct landline and from the explosions we could hear and the smoke we could see rising in a black cloud to the south-west.

That pall of smoke, although we did not know it at the time, was a presage of things to come, for it resulted from the first-ever kamikaze attack by a Japanese pilot. As though the damage to the aerodrome was not enough, we subsequently learned that a pilot had deliberately flown his Zero directly into one of a group of oil storage tanks belonging to the Royal Navy, and the fire lasted for three days.

160

We shall never know whether the aircraft had already been fatally damaged in the air-to-air fighting or whether the pilot deliberately chose suicide, perhaps because he had overstayed his endurance and had not enough petrol to regain the carriers. But this action must have inspired the later development of kamikaze squadrons whose pilots literally prepared themselves for immortality before taking off to hurl themselves and their planes into American aircraft carriers.

Certainly, the attack which began with the high-level pattern bombing from twin-engine bombers protected by a screen of fighters soon became a free-for-all at all altitudes, with the Japanese fighters using their machine guns on ground targets, including the two large main hangars. Unfortunately, between these hangars there was an ammunition dump, whose explosion wreaked more havoc than the direct bombing. In another incident, a low-flying Zero shot up a Hurricane as it force-landed, fatally wounding Flight Lieutenant Edsall as he strove to extricate the wounded pilot.

But these details only came to me next day, when I was able to visit China Bay and the naval hospital. For the present, I was hopping in and out of the R lorry, watching the plot of the receding attacking force and maintaining a one-man visual watch on the skies, all the while insisting that all other personnel kept under cover—particularly that our platoon of Ceylonese should stay in their trenches and NOT open fire unless attacked. I wanted our presence to stay undetected if at all possible.

Thus it was that, when the raid appeared to be finally over, I was standing alone in the open between the T and R towers when a single Japanese aeroplane came flying over from landward at just above treetop height. It was cruising along at no great speed, perhaps only 150 feet up, as though on a pleasure flight, and I hoped it would pass out to sea just north of us and leave us undetected.

But no, we had been spotted. He dropped the starboard wing tip, opened the throttle and came around in a tight turn to circle the T mast, so close that I could see the pilot's face, slit eyes and all, through his Perspex. It was a unique moment: in the whole course of the war; never before nor after did I see a real live enemy face-to-face, and neither, for that matter, did the vast majority of the millions of fighting men on both sides. The bomb or bullet that killed and maimed came from an unseen hand.

What I should have done, of course, was to fling myself as quickly as possible into my trench under the palm trees. Instead, I found myself sidling slowly towards cover, trying to look unconcerned and unnoticed, much as one might try to avoid being recognised and drawn into unwanted conversation by a casual acquaintance in a crowded street.

But reality soon took over and I was fully expecting the plane to come in again from seaward with machine guns blazing, for he had unquestionably identified us as a target. I scuttled quickly behind the nearest coconut palm and drew my pistol, only to see him complete the 360 degree turn and wing his way out to sea.

Aerial view of Trincomalee T and R towers

162

Perhaps his ammunition was all spent, perhaps his petrol was already overspent; I shall never know. But one thing is certain—our exposed and unprotected position on the beach was now known to the enemy.

The sound of the engine faded into the distance and peace descended again on our sunlit sea and palm-fringed shore; peace, that is, clouded by the knowledge that just over the horizon lay a flotilla of aircraft carriers whose planes would, in all probability, be rearming and refuelling to come back and finish us off.

It was no time to sit idly by and wait to be shot at. I mustered all the off-duty hands and set them to work on camouflage. Already we had attempted to sand-bag in the R lorry up to head height for the operators, and we now tried to cover the whole with palm and palmyra fronds, as well as the diesel generators and the T lorry. We tried to obscure the tracks left by the lorries coming on site and made a new access track under cover of the coconut plantation. But the two masts stuck out like sore thumbs and we even tried to obscure the outlines of these by tying palm branches across them and onto the guy ropes and wire stays.

Fortunately, these pathetic efforts were never put to the test, for the enemy had other fish to fry. They had, by chance, spotted *Hermes* as she fled to the south-southeast down the coast, and we were soon plotting the new attack as wave after wave of dive bombers sent her to the bottom where she lives to this day off Batticaloa, an officially designated war grave.

For us, the anxious day wore on as we hourly expected further attacks or even a full-scale invasion. Our fears were obviously shared by the native population, who fled as soon as the first bombs fell—all day a stream of oxcarts, cattle and goats poured up the only road to the north, jostled by barefoot Sinhalese and Tamils, young and old, carrying their household chattels on their heads. Every sort of craft, catamarans and rafts crowded with natives, fled up the coastal waters past our station towards Nilaveli and Mullaitivu.

By nightfall, the entire native population of Trincomalee numbered less than 100, or so we were told by the local police, and the next few days were to show us that this was so, for all the civilian servants of the various naval and military services had decamped and our food supply just stopped. The lorry I sent into China Bay came back with no provisions and only a report on the bomb damage which had, among other things, wiped out the MT section. It was perhaps as well that my driver came back before some senior officer requisitioned his lorry.

With no locally produced food, we were down to our reserves of bully and biscuits, and it was clear that one sack full didn't go very far among 50 men and so, having no adjutant, I decided to go off myself to China Bay to pull rank on the flight sergeant in charge of the cookhouse. I was offsite, and therefore in theory not to blame although I had had a nod and a wink beforehand: a poor deserted calf which the men had found wandering after the native exodus was miraculously turned into veal with a shot from a .38 revolver. When I got back to camp the meal was ready and all traces of the murder had been burnt.

At China Bay I found the destruction every bit as bad as had been reported. Out of the rubble of the MT section a brown-skinned leg was sticking, the body still unrecovered 24 hours after the bombing. A working party under the SWO, all wearing gas masks despite the tropical heat, were recovering other bits of bodies too small for identification or proper burial and incinerating them with petrol. It was no time for niceties and hygiene took precedence over sentiment.

I did not, this time, report to the group captain but was very well received by the other senior officers in view of the exceptional early warning we had given. A word with Squadron Leader Louis settled the matter of our rations. He was a man who got things done and who could recognise that our working radar was more important than a razor.

164

There is nothing to compare with a few bombs for changing the whole atmosphere of an RAF station from a peacetime to a wartime outlook, in less time than it takes for the smoke to clear.

***

This is an appropriate time in my personal narrative to sit back and review, in the glorious certainty of hindsight, the strategic position of the Japanese on the afternoon of April 9, 1942.

We know now what they actually did. They withdrew from the Indian Ocean, with three carriers returning all the way to Japan for refitting and reequipping.

But why? True, they had failed to find and sink our battleships, but they had destroyed an aircraft carrier, two cruisers, two destroyers and over 20 merchant ships. The sinking of *Prince of Wales* and *Repulse* north of Singapore had shown that battleships without air cover were no longer anything to worry about, and what better bait to draw the eastern fleet out of hiding than to send the invasion force, (which was two days' steaming away in the Andaman Islands) against Ceylon?

It must have been apparent that we had no garrison capable of resisting a landing and that our defences were trivial compared with those they had so effectively overrun in Singapore. The only thing they might fear would be the return to the scene of our battleships operating under air cover, and they did not know that these heavy units were retreating to Africa.

The one vital new thing they had learned from the Trincomalee attack was that our defences were radar controlled and this, as the Battle of Britain had shown, meant that every Hurricane could be placed where it was wanted and when it was wanted.

It may fairly be claimed that this made every aircraft at least 20 times more effective. This twentyfold advantage is if anything an understatement, as may be readily seen if one considers the radarless alternative: at very best, we could only have kept two aircraft at a time flying patrols at 20,000 feet, and with a visual range of say five miles this would be useless for early warning against a high-level attack which might come from any point in the compass.

We now know that the Japanese fleet did not themselves have any radar. It was not therefore the strength and fighting part of a handful of Hurricanes which surprised them: it was the fact that they were intercepted at all, making Trincomalee so vitally different from Colombo and Pearl Harbor. Their salad days were over.

There can be no doubt that, had the Japanese followed up their attacks with landings in Ceylon and India in the same way that they swept through Malaya to Singapore, they would have succeeded, and for some time Churchill and Roosevelt had to consider the awesome possibility of Japanese forces joining up with the Germans. Speaking of the spirited defence put up by the RAF in Ceylon, Churchill is recorded as saying of the Japanese: "They have come in contact with bone," and so they did.

Bone, indeed, in the form of the dashing bravery which took the young 261 Squadron pilots into battle against enormous odds, and all depended on them to snatch some sort of success out of what might well have been yet another terrible defeat.

I have chosen a different metaphor. While the British battlehorse was reeling in near defeat, with the British Empire itself open to invasion, one defiant kick was administered to Nagumo with an iron-shod British hoof. That vital kick came from the horseshoe of 261 Squadron, but in fact in the right place at the right time and that depended on just one Vital Nail. There had been no time to provide the other normal eight nails—indeed, there was only one, and that had been shoved into place by a totally inexperienced farrier, and at the last moment.

So Admiral Nagumo went into full retreat, just when we were at his mercy.

***

That same afternoon of April 9 I had my own worries: not only was I doing all I could to arrange some camouflage, but suddenly a new crisis broke—our landline to China Bay went dead. It was spine-chilling to think that we were scanning the skies over the whole eastern side of Ceylon and if we picked up an echo we could do nothing about it. We could not even telephone Squadron Leader Louis for help and still, for some reason, our WT contact had never been made to work.

It was do-it-yourself time again, and I shouted to LAC Robinson to bring a spare field telephone set, some wire, some pliers and a spike—any spike. From my own meagre resources, I contributed two darning needles and we jumped into the little Morris 8 and drove like mad along the jungle track, trying to work out the optimum strategy for finding the fault as soon as possible.

I knew there was some two miles of Don-8 wire lying in the jungle scrub beside the track, and to inspect every foot of it would take hours, so I drove as fast as possible to halfway or thereabouts and pushed the darning needles through the insulation of the cable, crocodile clipped them onto our field telephone and cranked the handle. My own station answered, so I knew that, in a little over two minutes, we had halved the search.

Two minutes later, and half a mile further up the track, I got an answer from China Bay. About turn and back towards the station, slower this time and trying to follow the green cable by eye through the undergrowth when we suddenly spotted a cut end, with a ten-yard gap to another cut end. The gap was soon bridged, and on our phone we checked continuity to both ends—Elizabeth Point was back on the air.

I was fortunate to have Robinson among my crew of mechanics and he could turn his hand to anything. Before night he had devised and manufactured out of wood and scrap metal an ingenious device rather like a pair of nutcrackers, which could be squeezed onto a telephone cable and which automatically punctured both lots of insulation and spiked in a pair of connections.

The events of the morning and the thought that our vital messages had all depended on this stretch of wire gave me much to think about. This was not a question of gnawing by wild animals (and it wasn't monkeys—the team had chosen not to hitch the wire up on the coconut trees just because the large population of langurs would swing on it); there were two clean cuts and a length just missing. It had to be a man's work, but who? Enemy agents? Fifth columnists? Japanese parachutists?

We had suddenly become important and so was our telephone line. I never knew from how high up the orders came, but work started straight away to dig two miles of trench and bury a new lead-covered cable all the way out to us. For immediate measures, the local police sent a posse. I went out with the officer while his men, all barefooted Malays, short, wiry and tough as nails, disappeared into the jungle trails in search of clues or informers.

There followed what to me was perhaps the most harrowing experience of the misfortunes of war. One of the men had picked up a tip and he led us on a long circuitous route which eventually led back to the beach down the coast. Here, in abject poverty and utter squalor, lived a poor fisherman with his wife and young children, the whole family in a wretched hovel made of bent twigs and a few tattered bits of Kadjan. Without ceremony, the barefoot policeman searched through the few tattered rags in the hovel, to emerge triumphantly with a length of Don-8 telephone wire which of course I had no difficulty in identifying.

I should have explained the field telephone cable type D8, still called Don-8 by the troops after the World War I telephone code which ran "Ack, Beer, Charlie, Don ..." comprised seven fine strands of strong steel wire and one strand of copper, the whole eight strands being covered in insulation, and two such insulated wires were lightly twisted together to make the cable. All my poor fisherman had done

168

was to help himself to a length to make fishing traces out of steel thread, bound with a pliable copper, an obvious and sensible thing to do, and I would gladly have given him some if he'd only asked for it.

What happened next horrified me, but I just had to stand by and watch, feeling horribly guilty and at the same time powerless. As soon as I had nodded my identification, the poor fisherman was seized and handcuffed to be dragged off to jail, whereupon his weeping wife and screaming children flung themselves to the ground and clung on to his legs in a vain effort to save their supporter and breadwinner.

The officer just shrugged his shoulders—he'd seen it all before and he was quite unmoved, and much as I felt sympathy with the poor wretch, I had to remember that we were ourselves fighting for our own lives. Once again it was no time for niceties, and with the fate of the British Empire hanging on my bit of field telephone cable, one could not worry about one poor fisherman; but I could not help feeling the injustice of it.

Chapter 12

Anxious days

The rest of April was a time of great anxiety although it seemed impossible that the Japs would not follow up their raids. At the very least we could expect renewed bombing, and I knew that our isolated spot on the beach had been pinpointed so we might well be a target.

Equally, a raiding party—even a handful of men from a submarine—could pick us like a ripe plum. My experiences taking Poonah to hospital before the raid had confirmed that not only were we outside the army's lines but the army just did not know we existed.

So I went off to Trincomalee and demanded an audience with the fortress commander. This did result in a face-to-face meeting with his deputy, a brigadier, who I asked what I should do and to whom I was responsible if we were attacked.

"Where are you?" he asked. I pointed out on the map our location and he burst out laughing. "That's where we're expecting the landing, and when it comes we're going to depress all our ack-ack guns and fuse them to burst out at head height all along the beach."

"Do I get a warning?"

"If it happens, it will be too late for you anyway."

Cold comfort! But at least the army as well as the navy and air force now knew where we were, and before long I was provided with a perimeter wire in the form of a triple dannert (concertina) wire all around the site. There were only two apertures: the main gate to landward and a small walk-through gap on the beach so that we could go swimming. All the good this would be in an attack would be to give us a line to cover with rifle fire and so, just possibly, a few more minutes in which to destroy our equipment.

Next I turned to my crew of airmen and found that only five of them had ever fired a rifle, so I gave these five a Lee Enfield each and kept the sixth for myself. My one incendiary round of .303 I kept in my pistol ammunition pouch, ready to fire into the petrol tank of the R lorry.

Not only were 90 percent of my men totally ignorant of firearms but they also seemed to lack any sort of basic disciplinary training. While their easy-going ways had done a splendid job in getting the station on the air, I was still much concerned that when the Japs landed, and we had to fight for our lives long enough to destroy the equipment and make for the jungle—why, then I should need to have my orders obeyed instantly.

I divided the nominal roll into two, straight down the middle by rank and craft or trade: half was to do all duties for 24 hours while the other half was given some basic training and the next day they were to change over. By the end of two days I hoped that all hands would have got the idea that I meant business.

Thus on the first morning I had some 25 men on parade in full marching order. I let it be known that their lives were likely to be short, very short if they didn't learn very quickly to jump to it, and that throughout the day they would be assessed so that they could learn from their own and other people's mistakes.

It was easy to find faults. The man on parade without a water bottle was soon made to look foolish, but a minute later his mates who had their bottles but had left them empty because it was less to carry had the smiles wiped off their faces. Who had lost his first field dressing? Who had not got his tin of emergency rations? It all went down on my score sheet.

I had them competing over 100 yards sprint, so that I could mark the last man home as dead and then I made them do it again in gas masks. Now this was highly unpopular, for a gas mask is a sweaty, cloying thing even in temperate climes, but in the tropics it is sheer hell.

Only one man, however, asked if he could be excused on the grounds that he was asthmatic, which gave me a splendid chance to say that I would be sure to let the Japanese know. The rest all saw the point that it was better to get a bit of experience before they came up against the real thing.

I invented a sort of wide game in the palm trees to see who was worst and best at improvising camouflage and avoiding detection. It was while this was going on and I was walking round umpiring that I had a dreadful fright: I was looking at one of my men as he crouched behind a tree when suddenly, in front of my eyes, an Indian soldier stood up from behind a bush, pointed a rifle into the man's back at point-blank range and fired.

My agonised shout, a split second too late, was drowned by the report of the gun. As I dashed forward in panic, the corpse stood up and started swearing at the wretched Indian, who was now shaking with fear himself. It had only been a blank round, and how were we to know that the Indians were having an exercise of their own over the same territory? But it lent an air of realism to our own training effort.

At the end of a long, hot, hard day I totted up all the black marks and designated about a quarter of my troops as dead, with another quarter as severely wounded. I read out the casualty list to all hands.

Next day we did the whole thing again with the other crew, and it was fascinating to see how the word had got around so that the second crew, for example, all had full water bottles—but I was able to introduce enough variety and change into the programme to ensure that I still had a lengthy casualty list, giving everybody something to think about.

I improvised a rifle range, using the Indian Ocean as a backing, so that all hands in turn would have the experience of firing a rifle under orders. In the middle of this someone drew my attention to a dark shadow, under the water out to sea. Shark? Submarine? Whatever it was, we fired a few rounds at it and it disappeared.

***

It was now some weeks since I had had any sort of news from home. One just lived from day to day, awaiting letters and placing one's faith in the thought that "no news is good news"; and then suddenly, on April 26 over my wireless loudspeaker came a shock. The Germans, in the second of the so-called Baedeker raids, had bombed the city of Bath.

The bold announcement of course gave no details, only that there were considerable casualties, and all I knew was that Peggy was there and might for all I knew at this very moment be lying under a heap of rubble. The next day the radio news said, "Bath was bombed again last night. Casualties are thought to be heavy. Several churches have been destroyed."

Happily, Peggy's lodgings were out of the city, and as I later learned her parents had hired a car next morning to take her to the relative safety of Gillingham. I sent an urgent, press-rate cable seeking news. The Allied propaganda machine made much of this attack as being a typically Hunnish act of barbarism against a purely cultural centre— but no doubt the Germans knew well that the Admiralty had been evacuated there from London and so it was a fair military target.

This was no comfort to me, and I listened to every broadcast describing the smoking ruins of the city with increasing alarm until, at last, I heard that she was safe in Gillingham. Her cable with this news took 11 days to reach me.

Slowly we began to get a little more civilised. My cabin trunk and bedroll arrived from Colombo, so I was able to revert to shorts and bush shirt again in place of the issue one-piece airmen's overall that I had been wearing. I had a tent to myself, right on the edge of the sand, under the last line of palm trees, with a mess table and a bench outside and my folding camp chair and my camp bed lit by a naked electric bulb.

My own tent

Elizabeth Point campsite

gone back to Colombo I sent him a signal to say I had found his missing equipment and would he like me to take it into my care?

My other visitor that week was the AOC himself, Air Vice Marshal D'Albiac, and he seemed to be a great deal more polite and even grateful for the performance of my unit during the Japanese raid.

On July 1 (which I noted in my diary as already the third anniversary of our unofficial betrothal) I was posted from my 272 MRU to 292 TRU to command. The official thinking was to erect first a mobile unit (we had done that and proved it in battle) and then a transportable unit (in huts, with fixed masts) and finally (if ever) a CO (Chain Overseas), a permanent, high-mast installation in permanent buildings, the counterpart of the CH or Chain Home station in England.

Thus it was that I had to start on a new assignment after only a few weeks of building my team of raw airmen into an effective unit. The copy of DROs issued on July 3 reads as follows:

272 AMES   Serial No 24
RAF   Page 1
Ceylon   Date 3.7.1942
            Daily routine Orders
        by Flying Officer EF Nielsen
        Commanding no 272 AMES

70 <u>COMMAND</u> Flying Officer EF Nielsen assumes command of No 272 AMES vice ..Flight Lieutenant B Samways w.e.f Ist July 1942
71 <u>PERSONAL MESSAGE</u> The following personal message from Flight Lieutenant B Samways is addressed to all personnel of No 272 AMES
"I would like to thank you all for your loyalty and hard work during the past months. The work you did at a particularly critical time is one of which you may always be justifiably proud. I wish you all the best of success

under your new commander and I am confident that you will uphold your present reputation in the future."

72   <u>Identity cards</u> A photographer will be arriving on the unit tomorrow, Saturday 4th July 1942, to take a photograph of all personnel for identity card purposes. All personnel are to hold themselves in readiness.

Signed EF Nielsen

Flying Officer commanding

272 AMES

Thus I passed on my command to Poonah but continued to live on the site and in fact to run the station. A young and inexperienced technical officer was sent up in whom Nielsen had no confidence, so Poonah just asked me what to do and then passed on my suggestions as orders. After a few days I caught the night sleeper to Colombo for a week of temporary duty, moving into the mess at 47 Kynsey Road with the other radar officers.

But there was nothing to do, so after a round of cinema visits and a bit of shopping at Cargills, where I bought a set of boxing gloves for the troops, I had a few minutes' interview with Floyd and then caught the night sleeper back to Trincomalee. As usual, I showed the conductor my gun before locking my compartment door and told him that if anyone came in in the night they would be shot. It was not unknown for sneak thieves to act in collusion with the train staff.

I repeated this trip three times in the next six weeks, which was in fact to be the total span of my new command although I did not then know it, and on one of these visits I was asked by one of my NCOs to try to get some oil lamp chimneys made of Jena glass.

This strange request had an interesting background and shows just how tenuous was the thread on which hung our defence of western civilisation. There we were, one solitary radar station to cover the whole eastern coast with no overlapping stations to allow the one hour a day maintenance luxury which the home chain stations had. If anything failed, it was a case of finding the fault, replacing the burnt-out part and getting back on the air as soon as possible—if we had a spare, that was.

On one occasion, I recall, the goniometer spindle seized up. We kept on the air for range only while I attacked it with a sledgehammer to draw the shaft, and then a file, by guesswork, until it would rotate again.

But to get back to the lamp glasses: one vital part of the transmitter was the high-voltage condenser which alone isolated the 20,000 volts DC which generated our output signal, holding back this lethal high voltage and allowing to pass out to the aerials only the ultra-high frequency radio pulse. Now we used bare wire feeders to the aerials and it only needed this condenser to fail in order to kill any of us who was touching the feeders or aerials, or even working on the mast, as we frequently were.

Each condenser comprised a single, thin glass separator between metallic plates, and this one-eighths-of-an-inch of glass alone shielded us from a 20,000 volt shock. After two such failures we had no more spares left and the next crack-over meant that we were off the air for good.

One of my NCO mechanics devised a way of making a substitute by soldering silver paper from cigarette packets onto the inside and outside of an oil lamp flue glass, the best heat-resistant type being those made in Jena, a source of supply not open to us in view of the war with Germany.

The native market in Trincomalee had yielded its last pair of glasses and one of these had cracked in the soldering, so we were down to rock bottom when I made my next trip to Colombo, where I promptly went down to the Pettah with a corporal mechanic and began enquiries. Now the Sinhalese will say "Yes master" in reply to every question even when the right answer is "No master" ("Are you a complete moron?" "Yes master"), so we went from stall to stall, attracting a tail of children and hangers-on until finally my corporal seemed to have made himself understood and we were promised that, if we waited, our little stallholder would "go see his friend" and come back with "one dozen glasses, yes Sir, one dozen, Sir, Jena glasses, Sir, very good".

We waited and sweated in the noonday heat and swatted the flies and listened to the babble of the crowd, until he came back with a dusty cardboard box holding a dozen lamp glasses. As a matter of principle, I offered half the money he was asking, which he accepted just a trifle too willingly.

I was just handing over the notes when my corporal said "Hold on, Sir, these aren't genuine Jena glass," and sure enough, the little etched word was a false lookalike.

"Jena Glass!" I shouted, and promptly drew my .45 automatic and pointed it straight at the stallholder's belly. The effect was dramatic. He grabbed the box and fled into the crowd, returning almost at once with the genuine article which he passed over without a murmur; he had known all along but was just trying to shift his inferior stock.

He even smiled as he took the money, but I kept my gun in my hand until we were both safely back in the staff car with our precious bits of German glassware needed to sustain our fight with Japan.

I now found myself in command of a handful of men (the nucleus of the staff of 292 TRU), various packing cases of equipment and a huge pile of timber in the shape of baulks of teak, big six-inch square timbers, drilled and numbered to take fishplates and bolts: the raw material for two self-supporting 120-foot-high towers.

The plan was for a team of Royal Engineers to be sent to build these for me, but they never came and so I just

180

set to and got on with it. The kindly and helpful "works and bricks" man from China Bay loaned me some native labour and a lot of cement. I already had a tape measure and a spirit level, so in pretty quick time I had four large holes dug for the four concrete footings of the first tower. The holding-down bolts for each foot had of course to be very accurately set up before being embedded in cement, with each foot on the corner of an exact 20 foot square. Never having built anything more ambitious than a rabbit hutch, I plunged into my task with foolhardy enthusiasm, solving any problems as they arose.

How to make an exact, 20 foot square? Use a slide rule to calculate the diagonal on the basis that the square root of two equals 1.414.

How to start a concrete mixer when the starting handle dogs have broken off? Get a long length of rope wound round the drum and 20 coolies to pull it with the engine in gear.

How to get a jib which had to be higher than the longest baulk? Go into the jungle and chop down a suitable tree.

How to turn radio operators into steeplejacks? Go up myself and show them it could be done. And thereby hangs a tale. A long time later, when I was visiting another station, I arrived on beer night and one of my old 292 team there was sufficiently lubricated to confide in me. "You know, Sir, I used to think you were a proper bastard, but when I saw you go up that mast like a monkey up a ... stick, I looked on you in a new light."

I was not to be allowed to see this enterprise through, and on August 30 I was posted to Colombo for a staff job, but the team of airmen I had founded completed the erection of both masts safely and went on to build several 184-foot self-supporting towers in the island for the new high tower COLs. I believe that some weeks later a team of REs actually arrived at Elizabeth Point to carry out the erection,

181

and Nielsen had the satisfaction of showing them the towers already standing.

"like a monkey"

Tower at Elizabeth Point

Chapter 13

Staff Officer

No sooner had I reached Colombo than I was off again to complete the erection of a mobile unit at Galle, within the ramparts which comprised the old Dutch fortress guarding Galle Harbour, a natural inlet at the extreme south of the island. Next day saw me at Mutwal, north of Colombo, where the first COL had been installed, and the day after that I was back at Elizabeth Point, having driven across the island at first light.

I worked all day and all through the night to get the new receiver on the air by 10 am, then back again to Colombo. It was of course foolhardy to drive again after 36 hours without sleep, and I nearly paid the penalty, for I fell asleep at the wheel—happily on a straightish stretch of jungle road, and I woke up with a start as my nearside wheels left the road, the jolting making my eyes open just in time to see the trees looming up and to swerve back onto the track.

It was now September and some reinforcements had reached the island. There was a mad scramble to get the radar cover extended as quickly as possible and a new MRU was formed in Colombo, with largely new personnel but under my old Trinco number of 272 AMES.

By good fortune, some of my own Trinco 272s had survived into this new unit, including Les Robinson, Johnny Fox and Jim Parry. I had by now acquired a reputation for getting things done, and I was given the task of getting this station installed at Batticaloa as soon as possible—or sooner.

Batticaloa is some 70 miles down the coast from Trincomalee, in the middle of Eastern Province, and about its only claim to fame is that a single track branch railway line reaches it through the jungle. There was no continuous coast road either north or south, and the cross-country road was meant for nothing faster than a bullock cart, but 272 MRU had to be set up there as soon as possible to plug the enormous radar gap between Trincomalee and Galle.

As usual, a new Japanese attack was expected at any time. As soon as we had loaded a few tents and some iron rations, armed with a map and a grid reference I led off my convoy of heavy lorries and trailers with perhaps 20 airmen—some on top of the stores, some in the lorry cabs and the rest in my Chevrolet station wagon.

It was the afternoon of Sunday September 13. Now the obvious routes out of Colombo go either north or south, and I soon realised that I was leading my armada on the wrong road and needed to be heading to the east. One cannot do U-turns with heavy lorries and trailers on a narrow native street fronted by boutiques, so I took the first turning left and hoped for the best. This cross street was even narrower and slummier, but it proved to be just wide enough to get through and there was no going back.

Unfortunately, it was not high enough, with electric street lights strung on wires across from one hovel to another, much lower than the overall height of our trailers. Where I led, the troops followed, and we cut a swathe through the lighting system, wires snapping and sizzling and broken glass everywhere. We never stopped, and I never heard any more about it.

Around midnight I called a halt and we just slept, where we were, in our clothes, huddled in the vehicles until first light. The Chevrolet would not start, but one of the mechanics soon found that the cut-out relay had stuck so that the battery had been discharging all night and it needed a tow start. But soon we were off, traversing the lower slopes of the high mountainous central region and with superb views across the mist-laden jungle into the rising sun.

Convoy to Batticaloa

The two best things for raising the morale of troops are hot food and a wash in fresh water. So when we came to the Diyaluwa Falls, where there is a sheer drop of 570 feet, I allowed all hands to wash in the icy water while our C and B fried tinned bacon on a petrol cooker. Our next mishap was that one lorry lost all its oil with a leaking sump. Happily, I managed to buy a drum from a little native shack, almost the only source for 100 miles. The RAF still owes me 7.20 rupees for this, which I paid out of my own pocket.

Diyaluwa Falls

The next difficulty was a deep ravine, bearing a sizeable river and spanned by an obsolete wooden trestle bridge bearing a notice "maximum working load two tons". It was a matter once again for intuitive mechanical engineering, for I knew that a lorry and trailer weighed over 10 tons and there was no detour possible, so it just had to be tested.

I examined the timbers carefully without getting much reassurance, for they were clearly very old. I considered whether it was sensible to just make a dash for it but rejected the idea in favour of feeling our way with a single lorry, detaching the trailer to be hauled over later on a long rope. I briefed the driver very carefully to go dead slow and to reverse if I shouted, then I climbed down the gorge to observe the trestles myself as the load came on.

They bent, they creaked and they seemed to sink by an inch or more, but there was no sudden collapse and I breathed again. Having seen the trailer safely towed over, I was confident that the rest of the convoy could follow in the same way and I drove on ahead to reconnoitre the site at Batticaloa.

I soon had a reason to regret this, for as dusk approached I still had one lorry missing. Was it lying in the ravine, a tangled mess of metal? With some apprehension I set off to drive the 60 miles back to the bridge, looking all the time to see if the lorry was coming towards me and getting more and more concerned as it failed to do so.

Finally, the bridge came in sight—yes, still standing—and there was the lorry, safe and sound but unable to start with a mechanical breakdown. It had to stay overnight until we could arrange a tow-in with a lorry from Batticaloa.

The site chosen for us was a sandy, scrub covered wilderness, and before we could get the heavy gear onto it we had to build a railway sleeper track using local resources including a working elephant. There was, of course, no properly defined boundary to our site which nearly caused trouble, for no sooner had the tents been pitched on a reasonably open space nearby than an indignant party of natives came to complain. We had made camp in the middle of their cemetery.

Work proceeded apace and by Saturday evening the R mast was ready for hoisting. Since the Sunday morning dawn raids on Pearl Harbor and Colombo, we were especially alert on every Sunday and feast day in the calendar, so we pressed on and hoisted the mast after dark. Next morning the T mast was erected and we worked all that day and far into the night, beyond the limits of prudence and even of our endurance. The last I remember of Sunday September 20, 1942 was desperately trying to trace a wiring fault in the receiver lorry, together with two mechanics.

Building the approach road to Batticaloa

Batticaloa campsite

I awoke, stiff and cold, just as dawn was breaking and found myself lying awkwardly on the floor of the wagon. Slumped beside me were the R mechanics, both sound asleep. In my stiff fingers I still clutched a hot soldiering iron. And so we failed in our "on the air by dawn" effort but by only a few hours, and by 15.00 hours I could report 272 fully operational and repair to the rest house for a bath and a sleep.

**

The next morning, I left by the up-country route to visit Namunukula where Tony Blanco-White was in charge of a COL. This was a unique site, for although it was 40 miles inland it was on the very edge of the uplands at an altitude of 4000 feet. The height gave it exceptional low-flying coverage, far outweighing the 40 miles loss of range, and it plotted ships as well as aircraft at zero feet right around the eastern seaboard. This was of enormous importance and soon gave rise to an attempt to provide similar cover in Colombo in the west; but more of that later.

On this first visit I did not stay, although the tea plantation at Kandahena was a wonderful relief from the heat and humidity of the coast, and I pressed on as far as Belihuloya to the rest house for a night's sleep and an icy cold swim in a mountain stream next morning.

The rest of the year, 1942, was spent in constant travel and constant work, still a full seven days in every week, dedicated to siting, installing and servicing a ring of stations around the island from Trincomalee to Colombo.

Two adventures during this time are worthy of record, apart from minor incidents like seeing a leopard and running over an enormous snake as thick as a drainpipe. The jolt nearly broke the car springs, but the reptile slithered off regardless.

The adventures concern the insect life of Ceylon, which could indeed be more perilous than the larger wild beasts. In the first incident I had to go down to Galle with a young officer named Tapscott to erect another 105-foot mast. As soon as I saw this I condemned it on the spot, for it had been locally made in India out of very poor wood and I much doubted if it would support its own weight.

As usual, there was a panic on and we had another deadline to meet, so I decided to go and get the original 272 mobile mast from Trincomalee, now superseded by 292 TRU. We left at once for Colombo, Tapscott driving the old Morris 10 staff car with the windscreen hinged wide open— a facility which many cars of the 1930s had. I was in the passenger seat.

Staff car with hinged window

In through the front flew a single hornet, to bounce off Tapscott's head and end up on my forearm, where it stung me. The pain was both immediate and excruciating, but we were glad that it was only the passenger and not the driver who suffered, and I did not then have the sense to report sick and we just pressed on: a quick rest in Colombo, off again through the night to Trincomalee, working all the next day to see the mast down and loaded and then another night drive, with one driving and one sleeping in two-hour spells.

It was common for native bullock carts to plod through the night, without lights of course, and often with the driver sleeping. One of these was hit a glancing blow, his axle cutting a gash in the front wing and the bang waking me up smartly. It was not only fatigue I was suffering from, for by now my whole forearm was swollen up like an outsized rugby ball and the site of the sting itself was a suppurating mess.

But we pressed on, getting to Colombo at 2 am and sleeping until breakfast, then off again to Galle where within 24 hours we got the new mast safely erected. Another all-night effort and I had 209 MRU on the air by 6 am on Saturday, November 7. My swollen arm persisted for another three months until finally the wound itself seem to rot and fall out to leave a pit half an inch across and nearly as deep. I still have the scar. (I later learned that a single such thing would kill a child and half-a-dozen would kill a man. I did not doubt it.)

Galle ramparts

My other tangle with insect life was, fortunately, not of such a lasting effect but was even more painful. It happened while we were on a trip to find a site in the wild country between Batticaloa and Trincomalee. We had left the staff car where the track petered out and taken to our feet, and the compass, to push through the undergrowth until we struck the sea.

Going east on a compass to hit the Indian Ocean is one thing; but going west to try to find a camouflaged car in the jungle is quite another matter, and so I climbed the tallest tree I could find to look for a sighting point in land, which seemed at the time to be a good idea.

When I realised that I was being bitten by some fierce-looking brown ants, I made the error of thinking that if I climbed on up, and quickly, I should get above them. No hope! In a matter of seconds, I was covered all over in a horde of biting insects, inside my shirt and shorts, my stockings and shoes, my hair, my ears—everywhere.

In agony and yelling with the pain, I fell out of the bottom branches and dashed for the sea, flinging off what clothes I could on the way before plunging into the warm salt water. Even underwater they still clung and bit, but without clothes on it was possible to splash and slap them away. My companions had a good laugh.

Chapter 14

Parantan and Kilinochchi

The northern province of Ceylon is all low-lying country, and it was thought that an MRU in the area might give cover over the seas surrounding the Jaffna peninsula. So once again, at the end of November I found myself taking off with another untrained and newly formed unit, 296 AMES, bound for a grid reference called Parantan.

We made Anuradhapura after dark, and here was a small garrison of East African troops under British officers. They kindly gave me and my men a billet for the night, and by next afternoon we were leaving the only proper road and trusting our heavy lorries to the stony track, across the scrub, meant for nothing bigger than a bullock cart. I found the site and we pitched tents for the whole unit in the last hour of daylight.

Just before dawn the monsoon broke. In a matter of minutes my camp bed was standing in a lake, inside the tent, and at first light the awful truth became apparent: what had, in the dry, seemed to be an excellent, flat, dry patch of wasteland was a disused paddy field and the first rain of the season had turned it into a sea of mud.

For half a day we struggled to get the lorries onto the site and for the next day and a half we struggled to dig them out and get them back on the dirt road. For the time being, at least, it seemed to be impossible to get a mast up anywhere in the northern province.

In the next week I toured the area thoroughly up to Elephant Pass and across to Mullaitivu, interspersed with trips back to Colombo and down to Trincomalee, before selecting a field close to the tarmac road at Kilinochchi where I left the unit to make camp as best they could and took a night sleeper train for Colombo, having to share a sleeping birth with a dark skinned gentleman who spent most of the night crouched in a corner praying over a set of apparently sacred bony relics which he unwrapped from a dirty cloth.

December 22 was the full moon, and we were getting edgy about the possibility of an attack on Christmas Day, so with no news that 296 was yet working, I set off after dark to drive through the night and find out why. The sleeping camp was not expecting a visitation from headquarters when I plodded in through the mud at 5 am and flashed the torch into tent after tent until I found an empty bed, into which I flopped for an hour's sleep, regardless of whose it was.

The rightful owner (probably the duty guard who had failed to notice my arrival) came in after dawn and, surprised, let out the classic line, "'Ere, who's sleeping in my bed?"

I was not best pleased at being woken, and despite his "Sorry, Sir" when he recognised me, I could not help making the appropriate reply of "F… off, Goldilocks." He fled, no doubt to warn the officer in charge that the worst had happened, and I was in their midst again.

By the end of a long day I had the T mast up and the aerial rigged, so I allowed myself a night's sleep, leaving a skeleton crew to lay out the R mast during the dark hours, ready for an all-out effort on Christmas Eve. If it was at all possible I was going to be on the air by first light, mindful that it would be Christmas Day, and remembering the Japanese attack on Colombo on Easter Sunday, so we worked all day and we worked all night—and failed to make it by dawn. The troops wanted to relax but I would have none of it, and by teatime we got operational.

Surely, it was rumoured, Sam wouldn't insist on a night shift on Christmas Day. But Sam did, and the reluctant crew had to forgo their night of revelry.

Secretly, they knew I was right, and the protests, such as they were, were all good-humoured and no threat to discipline. One or two of the crew had been with me at Trincomalee and we knew each other well enough, and I was allowed to see and to have copies of their versions of the Parantan-Kilinochchi saga.

These contemporary writings are reproduced and edited, for they give, crudity and all, a true sample of the spirit and the wit shown by the airmen of those days. I think they show too the rather special relationships which we had in the air force across the boundaries of rank: they could lampoon me openly but without the slightest suggestion of indiscipline, and I was proud to command such men. Together we helped to win the war.

The first is a versified account from one of the Canadians who had come into Ceylon as reinforcements:

I ask you chaps, is it fair?

There's a lovely seaside place called Jaffna
That's noted for xxx shops and fun,
And 296 Unit stuck near there
To keep the Japs on the run.

When we arrived at the station
The sun was shining and bright.
There were only two things that we wanted,
A damned good meal and a shite.

The one we had in the dining tent,
The other, behind the trees,

196

Then the acting CO gave us a nice talk
To put us at our ease.

He said, "Now make yourself comfy boys,
There's not much to do in this dump.
When the convoy comes in this afternoon,
There'll be hard work, 'All hands to the pump'."

Then some of us rigged up a shit house
And put four new seats in a row,
While the others dusted the tent pegs
For Sammy was coming you know.

We didn't know what he would look like,
We expected a superman,
We found him an ordinary fellow
With a perpetual grin on his pan.

The CO was a Canadian
And therefore quite harmless you know,
And then he contracted dengue
When only two days on the show.

There was one nice site chosen for us,
We thought it looked reasonably good.
So we brought up our diesels and Gen wagons,
But the buggers got stuck in the mud.

"Oh, that's alright", says old Samways,
It's only the Crossley that's in
I'll drive up the Gen^2 wagon myself now"
And soon he put that bastard in.

And Sammy, he starts us to working

2
 Gen is an abbreviation of genuine and therefore meaning the real thing. Hence
"Gen wagon" meaning the transmitter or receiver lorry.

Like xxxx, not civilised chaps,
The station goes up regardless,
Of comfort, or grub, or naps.

We're out on parade in the morning,
Before the sun, it can rise,
And we work like the bloody Devil,
'Til the mossies replace the flies.

"And can we have some more bodies,
On the ludkin,[3] the sandbags and all.
We mustn't be behind schedule"
Is Sammy's perpetual call.

But soon there's a shout in the distance.
The fellows all cheer with great might,
For Jock's got the R wagon and diesel
And driven them safe to the site.

Sammy takes a hand at the driving
Of the Gen wagons and orders the sprogs
To get cracking a little faster
And stop acting like sleepy xxxx.

Everything looked, Oh, so rosy
Then the rain started doing its bit.
And the wagons sank one after t'other
And we dug them out of the shit.

Sammy he drives the T wagon
And his driving is simply grand
Everything goes lovely
Till the T wagon reaches the sand.

It sways about ever so grandly
When sitting up ever so high,

---

[3] Ludkin - a type of transmitting aerial named after a boffin at TRE.

Then slows down ever so quickly
And settles a-tilt with a sigh.

"And now for the base plates," says Sammy,
The Thorny was full to the top.
"We've put a few leaves on the roadway,
Get going and don't bloody stop."

So Jock did his best with the wagon,
He went up a hell of a way,
But the wagon sank to the axles.
We thought it was there to stay.

"All hands to unload this wagon," says Sammy
With a very sarcastic grin,
The fellows fall over each other
They're anxious you see to begin.

"There's snakes in these parts!" bellows Roscoe,
"There's some fellow going to be dead."
He stoops down and picks up a bastard
With his hands on its tail and its head.

He shows it around to the fellows,
It's Tic Polonga[4], you see.
"These little fellows need killing".
And he bashes its head on a tree.

But there's the sound of a shout in the distance,
The "Tiffin" is ready to serve.
The chaps would like to rush for it,
But it seems they haven't the nerve.

"All right, break for lunch," says our sergeant
And the men all whet their teeth.
They know they had sausage for breakfast

---

[4] Tic Polonga is a venomous snake

So now it will be corned beef.

They eat in less than 5 minutes,
And scarce can they turn about
Before Sergeant Miller is shouting
"Come on fellows, everybody out!"

So back once again to the puddle,
There's rain everywhere one can see.
"The mast goes up tomorrow," says Sammy,
His face, an expression of glee.

So the fellows filled eight hundred sandbags,
They worked against time in a race,
And when they got everything ready
A medical inspection took place.

The MO said he was sorry,
He'd have to condemn this spot
Sammy said, "Move the domestic site."
The MO said, "The whole bloody lot."

So off they went the next morning
And came back full of glee.
"We've found five acres, five miles away,
It's as dry, as dry can be."

The men weren't a bit excited,
They'd been had before you know.
And all they said to each other
Was " F... the whole bloody show."

So they grumbled and grumbled and grumbled,
The things they said you can guess.
It didn't make one bit of difference
They'd to start clearing up the mess.

But somehow they loaded the lorries

With beds and tents and kits.
By this time some fellows weren't feeling so well,
Developing attacks of the shits.

The rest of us stuck it and stuck it.
We've moved the domestic site.
The lorries were packed with beds and tents
About twenty feet in height.

And on the top sat the fellows,
Ducking to miss the trees,
And though there were smiles on their faces
They were on their f...... knees.

The xxxx, they build the roadway
On which the R wagon rides,
While lads are going to the sick bay
For mossies have bitten their hides.

And after we've finished the transfer
We start all over again,
Building the masts and the ludkin
And hope for relief from the rain.

The ranks are ever depleting,
Far more are reporting sick.
As long as we get their beer ration
The less reason we'll have to kick.

It was the night before Christmas,
When the weary but hopeful men
Said "Surely we'll get Christmas off,"
And Sammy, he just smiles again.

And what did really happen
When Christmas Day it arrived,
We were ruddy well operational,
Of holidays we were deprived.

Now we've got help from Colombo
Three ops, two mechs and two cooks.
So now we've got five Canadians
Who know their gen from the books.

Alas Mr Samways has left us,
The place doesn't seem quite the same
But guess when we least expect him
The -er-kind soul will show up again.

Results are really far reaching
And startling to everyone here.
Maybe we'll see Schickelgruber
When they place him in state on his bier.

On New Year, as you all know,
On watches we have to be,
Helping to bring a bit nearer
The "End" in '43.

But we'll put up with all these hardships
And we don't mind just a one or two more,
If we can be sure that in "Blighty"
We'll welcome '44.

***

The second version came from a radio operator who had
been with me at Trincomalee. He had been a schoolmaster in
civil life and was a good raconteur and wit, as the following
shows:

Here beginneth the first lesson:

Chapter 1 of 296th Book of AMES

And it came to pass that upon a certain day in the fourth year of wrath, a certain band of Raphites were driven forth from the land of plenty which was fourteen leagues from the Peak of Adam. Verily I say unto you were they cast out from the seat of slothful indolence where dwelt the Pharasites. The Thrice Two Group. Great was the wailing and great was the gnashing of teeth as these sons of misery and destitution were driven as by the whips of Pharaoh, from the dusky bosoms of their new found spouses. And the hand of the Thrice Two Group lay heavy upon them, albeit they knew not wherefore they had sinned. And along unknown paths were they forced to journey, far into the wilderness of Lanka. And after many days, wherein their heavy eyes knew not slumber, Seech the son of Can, who was their leader, halted the weary pilgrims. Verily I say unto you did these outcast Raphites pitch their tents and lay their weary heads to earth, wondering but understanding not.

And it came to pass that the sins of past transgressions were heavy upon the head of this Seech, Son of Can, and Dengue, the evil spirit, took possession of his body.

Dominion over them passed then into the hand of Greyoh, born out of wedlock, who knew not the ways of the company.

And after the going out of Greyoh, came Sam and with him came the winds of fury and the tongues of vipers. And like a tempest did he descend upon them. And Sam opened loud his mouth, as one having authority over them, and sainthood: "Verily shall ye, oh bodies, toil until the work of mammon be fashioned, nor shall he eat, nor shall he sleep until the work be done."

But the heavens opened, and the rains descended and the floods came and the winds blew and beat withal upon that craven flock. And, behold, they cried out with loud voice, saying thus: "Why cast ye us out from the land of plenty, and torment us, and place a yoke upon us?" Whereupon Sam spoke saying, "Oh Generation of Vipers, how can ye, being evil, expect good things?"

And verily did sons of man in bondage under the elements of the world, strive; but their striving was set at naught for it is not given to the son of man to perform miracles.

And it came to pass that upon the fourth day of the flood, there came into their midst one Emmo, a wise and learned man, who didst straightly command Sam and his servile men to take up their possessions and all their household goods and depart thence to a new land, lest grievous harm befall them, for a plague was rife upon that place.

Upon these words the servile host was filled with rejoicing and joy was manifest upon their countenance.

And, verily, to that place came certain elders of the tribe, among which was Floy, the high and mighty. This man was a chief scribe, a law unto himself. And when he was come there he was greatly affected lest he defile his feet and raiment with the mud and filth of that mighty flood which lay all about.

And it came to pass that Seech, the Son of Can, was made whole and he didn't come again amongst them who were his followers. And he led them out from that foul spot and the evils thereof,

Many were the trials and tribulations that beset them about before they entered into the village that was Kilininoch, where certain men of an unknown tribe had already taken up their abode. And exhorted as they were by Al Miller, a man of mighty voice, these serving men did pitch again their tents in the midst of a mighty flood. And like unto the slaves of Egypt were they made to travail, in weariness and hunger, to raise up to heaven two mighty towers like unto the Tower of Babel.

And it came to pass that divers of these serving men were tormented of an unclean spirit, yea, did they become as children, weak and sick of mind, so that Coo, who dealt in physic, took them as lepers from that place. And it came to pass that so great was the labour and so few were there to do it, that others of their tribe, that still dwelt in the marble halls in the land of plenty, were likewise forced to arise out of their licentious living and depart thence into the wilderness, to live in temperance and in hunger with their oppressed brethren.

Verily I say unto ye, if ye ask for an egg, shall ye be given a bull? Here endeth the first lesson.

Here beginneth the second lesson,

Chapter 2 of the 296th Book of AMES

And it came to pass, that, after many weary days wherein they were sore oppressed by the burden of their labours, these bond men, who were Raphites, builded up two mighty towers unto the heavens. Whereupon they were exceeding glad, and dids't sigh heavy sighs for at last was the work of mammon performed. And there was great joy for the day of feasting was at hand.

And it came to pass that upon this holy day, even as they sat to the feasting, the presence of Sam, of evil countenance, dids't come upon them as an icy blast, and their light was turned to darkness. And verily were the joints of their limbs loosed so that their knees smote one against the other. And the wrath of Sam descended upon them as a tempest, and he opened loud his mouth and didst pronounce judgement upon them. And he spake thus saying: "Mine eye will not spare ye, neither will I have pity." And upon these words they, that were as hirelings, cried out saying, "Wherefore are we counted as beasts and reputed vile in thine eyes?" But Sam heeded not their entreaties and silenced their lamentations at a word, and verily did he speak thus saying, "Though ye cry out in mine ears with a loud voice, I will not hear ye, for my word is law."

And their hopes were as the giving up of the ghost. And as they trembled and feared before him, six bodies which were evil in his sight were taken from the feast and cast out. And, behold, were they thrown into utter darkness and made to revolve a mighty wheel, even as the beasts of the field. Thus was sacrifice made to appease the wrath of them that dwelt in the marble halls of plenty, they that were called the Thrice Two Group.

But there came a day which was turned unto them from sorrow to joy, from sadness to gladness. And that day was the day wherein the sojourn of Sam, the taskmaster, was brought to an end.

And it came to pass, that Sam with his chariot of fire departed thence to the city of plenty, to sit again on the right hand of Floy, that was the greatest of all of them that dwelt in the marble halls.

And at his going there came an end to the rain and the floods ceased and peace came upon the village that was Kilinochchi. And upon that day, verily I say unto you there was rejoicing: and in thanksgiving did the Raphites host lift up loud their voices. Verily did they fill with wine their drinking vessels and raise up their voices in song to the music of a reeded pipe.

But it came to pass that a famine descended upon the Raphites and evil spirits brought destruction among them, so that many were they that were carried off weak and sick as of a palsy. And among them that were possessed of an evil spirit was Seech, the Son of Can, he that was their leader. And verily did he depart thence to be ministered by one Emmo, a caster out of devils.

And of the scribes, next in order to Seech, came Soo, a mighty hunter that was strong of arm and quick of eye. And to this Soo, who was famed throughout the land as a slayer of dogs, was passed dominion over them.

Many were the afflictions that beset these exiles about; and wild beasts of the wilderness and fowls of the air did come to add to their evils so that they were oppressed: verily I say unto ye were their tents and dwelling places filled to overflowing with frogs and doleful creatures. Truly were the unwary damned.

And it came to pass that the weary host did thirst for water and didst cry out in their sufferings; but Tom called Taff, he that dwelt alone, didst raise up his voice in authority saying: "Heed ye that ye drink not of the waters lest ye be taken of the plague." And so many were the trials and so great were the tribulations of that company of Raphites that many were they that were smitten of a wanderlust and didst depart to new lands. Verily I say unto ye, that out of every two of the pilgrims that journeyed into the wilderness of Lanka but one did remain; so that the remnants of the flock were left, forsaken by their fellow men to travail in watchings and fastings unto the day of salvation.

Verily I say unto ye, if you ask for the fruit of thy labour, shall ye be given a lemon?"

Here endeth the second lesson.

Chapter 15

1943: The Defensive Build-up

So passed 1942, a year in which we made frantic efforts to try to improvise radar cover around the harbours of Colombo and Trincomalee in the face of overwhelming enemy sea and air supremacy. For me, it had been a time of unremitting personal effort, working seven days a week and many nights as well, with not even Christmas Day (especially not Christmas Day) as a day off duty.

It took its toll, and in early January I found myself with a high fever. I did not willingly take to my bed, but by midday I could no longer stand and I was violently sick. Illnesses in the tropics move at an alarming pace and I had already seen colleagues die within hours from polio and from blackwater fever.

After 24 hours of vomiting I was committed to 35 Base General Hospital at Mount Lavinia, diagnosed as having both dengue fever and infective hepatitis. For a whole week my sole diet was dry toast and glaubers salts; effective indeed but not calculated to raise morale, and I scarcely cared whether I lived or died. No-one came to see me; no mail; no-one at home even knew I was in hospital.

For a week I starved, shivered and sweated until my temperature dropped to double figures and I was allowed a mouthful of steamed fish. Although anxious to get back to work, I was ordered to go on 14 days' sick leave, arranged through my good friend Percy Gaddum. A tea planter himself, he was secretary of the Tea Planters' Association but was commissioned into the RAF for his local knowledge, and he and I had made many trips together into the jungle. Now he arranged for me to stay privately with Gordon Allday on his beautiful estate at Nawalapitiya. Gordon, whose family had been evacuated to South Africa, was glad of the company and gave me a splendid convalescence.

I had to pass a medical board before returning to duty. Pronounced fit, I decided that I would now work only six full days in a week, and by and large I managed to take one day, or two half days, off in each week.

We now became part of 222 Group proper, with our "radio" (that is, radar) office on the topmost floor of the Secretariat building in Colombo. Under the senior radio officer, Willy Floyd, there were eight of us, R1, R2, etc down to the most junior, R8. I found myself appointed R1, the senior technical officer and therefore de facto deputy to Floyd.

222 Group at Galle Face

We of the radar staff had a mess of our own, which included a number of filter officers for the Colombo filter room and I was the PMC (President of the Mess Council) which meant that everyone did as they liked but I was responsible.

Floyd, however, continued to live in the Galle Face Hotel and did not mix with us socially at all. To us, he always seemed to be conscious of his superior rank and although there was no doubt he had done a great deal to organise a radar system, he worked very much as a staff officer, leaving the likes of me to get our hands dirty at the sharp end. Maybe it was our fault, but somehow a gulf developed between the SRO and Rs 1 to 8, and poor R1 became a Christian to Willy Floyd's Bligh.

Of course I never led a mutiny or anything remotely like it, but I was probably then, as now, tactless enough not to conceal my lack of respect for superior badges of rank, just because they were superior, if I did not think their wearers were better men than me.

It all came to a head one day when Willy telephoned from the Galle Face Hotel and demanded his staff car be sent round at once. I found it was not available for some reason and the only transport under my direct command was that in which we junior officers rode to work every day: a requisitioned, open sided little native omnibus, hastily painted in green camouflage and known to us all as "the xxx bus". I sent that.

According to the driver, who reported to me afterwards, the Senior Radio Officer was NOT AMUSED, and he was given to understand that this bus was not again to approach the august portals of the Galle Face. Maybe it was coincidence, but next day I found myself effectively demoted to a role as a trainer of 0R radio operators, in a written memo signed by the SRO and countersigned by a wing commander for the Staff Officer Admin. My diary note on that day reads "and the hand of thrice two group lay heavily upon him, though he knew not wherefore he had transgressed".

I carried on as though nothing had happened, and in fact the very next day I was off to the Koggala whence I flew in a Catalina down to Addu Atoll in the Maldive Islands, to

210

inspect the station there, then on to Diego Garcia and back to Koggala. In the next weeks I flew and motored (and sometimes walked) into many inaccessible corners of the island, including Kandloya (of which more later) and Kankesanturai in the extreme north.

I also put in a formal application for posting away from 222 group, which had to be considered by the SPSO. I shall never know what lobbying or counter-lobbying went on, but the facts are that I stayed and Willy Floyd was posted to India.

His replacement, Squadron Leader Reg Parry, had been a regular airman in peacetime, and he and I were firm friends for the rest of his short life. I seemed to be R1 again and we got on with the war, putting in new stations all over the island and updating and improving the original ones as more and better equipment became available. But no one, so far, had solved the problem of Kandloya, which became known as Floyd's Folly. This is the whole story.

I had had nothing to do with the siting or commissioning of the four low-flying (COL) stations which were now operating in the island, having been fully occupied with the pioneering MRUs and the TRUs which replaced them. I therefore escaped all blame for the total failure of Kandloya, on which there was now an inquest.

But to begin at the beginning we have to go back to the experiment, for which Floyd deserves all credit, of siting a 1.5 metre wavelength, low-flying COL at a height of 4000 feet at Namunukula. It was a great success, plotting aircraft at ranges up to 200 miles around the eastern coast as well as shipping.

Immediately, the need for a similar station covering the southwestern seas around Colombo was apparent, but the mountains did not have the same suitable topography. Undeterred, Willy had selected a jungle-covered mountaintop at Kandloya and expended enormous manpower on overcoming the logistical problems. As high up into the tea country as there was any sort of track, a hutted camp was built for the personnel.

211

As the rainfall at this spot was the highest in Ceylon at over 300 inches annually, it was not a pleasant place to live and work. From this camp a proper road had to be built, involving the felling of half a mile of jungle up a jagged, rocky ridge. Eventually the job was done and the station was declared operational, with 24-hour shifts of men gazing at a cathode ray tube showing nothing but a few permanent echoes from the surrounding mountains.

All the best technical brains in the island (except me) visited the station and pored over the equipment. They found no fault, but still the tube showed no aircraft.

This was the situation which Parry inherited from Floyd—an enormously expensive flop. His own solution to the problem was to blow it up with dynamite, on the improbable grounds that the mountains must be full of magnetic ore which stopped it from working, but before taking this final step he discussed it with me and I offered to have a last look.

This was a case of a fool rushing in where angels fear to tread, for I was acutely aware that my knowledge and experience of radio transmitters and receivers was rudimentary compared with those of other technical officers and NCOs. All I had to rely on was a basic knowledge of physics and a lot of cheek.

The type of COL installed, at a fantastic cost in money and effort, was the latest type with a single, continuously rotating aerial array which both transmitted the pulse of energy and received the returning weak echo a few microseconds later. The signal picked up on each of the 20 pairs of dipoles was passed in phase to a common feeder leading to a tiny circular coil, rotating with the aerial array and feeding the radio-frequency signal by induction to a fixed coil on the same axis, so eliminating the need for slip rings. The signal then passed through high-frequency and intermediate-frequency amplifiers until it was big enough to show up on the cathode ray tube.

The type and frequency (200 megacycles) of Kandloya were the same as those of Mutwal, the coastal

COL north of Colombo at sea level, and I made one little observation which no one else had spotted and which I kept to myself for the time being. This was that every time the transmitted beam from Kandloya swept over Mutwal, Mutwal tube was momentarily saturated, whereas the similar beam sent out from Mutwal did not saturate Kandloya when it passed.

I argued to myself that, whatever the reflecting surface was like between the stations, at least it was exactly the same for the one as for the other, and therefore if Mutwal's direct beam did not saturate Kandloya then it must be the receiving system and not the transmitter which was faulty. This halved the problem area, but in fact I already knew that the later stages of amplification were normal as these had been tested with the input of a signal generator.

Armed with this foreknowledge and accompanied by a sergeant mechanic and a spare, complete, radio-frequency amplifier, I drove up the mountain from the coconuts to the rubber trees and on through the tea plantations to the jungle-clad mountaintop. In the Ops room the crew were faithfully watching a blank tube, as they had now been doing for weeks on end ("wondering and understanding not", I thought). It was a few minutes' work to fit in the new RF amplifier and this gave no improvement, so it MUST be lack of an input signal.

I went out and onto the gantry, riding round and round over the treetops on the aerial array as it rotated continuously, and personally checked each pair of dipoles to see that they fed each one to its right feeder line, until I was down to a single pair of feeders disappearing into the centre of the turntable, on the way to feed their signal to the rotating coil.

Now I knew that any coil would show a high resistance when fed with alternating current but should show no resistance to a direct current, so I put an ohm-meter across the two feeders and got—infinity! Eureka!

Without saying anything of this to the crew, I went down to the Ops room and asked for a hot soldering iron.

Sure enough, one of the wires feeding one end of the tiny concealed coil was not making contact: the fault must have been in the equipment from its manufacture in England. I dabbed on a blob of solder and at once the tube sprang to life, showing the outline of the coast with Colombo Harbour and ships at sea, and aircraft 100 miles away. It was a sweet triumph.

The aerial gantry at Kandloya

By the end of the year we had established a radar ring around the important areas of the island, with both high-level and low-level cover and with filter rooms at both Colombo and Trincomalee. Neither were we neglected by the enemy, for although the threat of a full-scale invasion seemed to have faded and no more carriers entered our seas, we were reconnoitred by four-engine flying boats whose method of operation was to come across the Indian Ocean. No doubt they were also able to give guidance to their submarines.

On the November full moon we plotted this intruder all around the coast from Galle to Colombo, with sufficient accuracy and length of warning to get a Beaufighter scrambled from Vavuniya. We stood in the filter room and watched the converging plot with the mounting excitement and cheered madly when we heard that the intruder had been shot down, and then we opened the bar in the mess for an impromptu party, singing and rejoicing at the deaths of the Japanese crew.

Next day, in the Intelligence Section at Group HQ, I saw the official photos of the corpses, again with no compunction. In conversation with the duty intelligence officer, I found him puzzled as to why the flying boat had had a feed of "soda water" to its petrol tanks: After going into alternative translations for the Japanese inscriptions I was able to advise him that it was, in fact, a carbon dioxide gas feed, used to replace air from the emptying petrol tanks so that they would not be liable to explosion in combat.

Chapter 16

1944: The Offensive Build-up

We entered upon 1944 in a fairly optimistic mood, for the war seemed at last to be running in our favour. Italy had capitulated, and both the Germans and the Japanese had been forced to some extent to retire from their forward positions. At home, we knew preparations had been going on for a long time with the aim of a second front—that is, the landing in northern Europe which eventually came on June 6, while the Americans were painfully and painstakingly island hopping across the Pacific.

In Ceylon, our new large and flourishing radar system was taken out of 222 Group and formed into 183 Wing (with its HQ at the Colombo Golf Course clubhouse) and we became part of Air Command, South East Asia and therefore passed into the overall command of the Supremo, Admiral Lord Louis Mountbatten.

Almost imperceptibly, we found we had drifted out of the heady buccaneering days of 1942, back to a more organised air force where junior officers like mere flight lieutenants had to do what they were told. This was not entirely to my liking, and more than once I found myself in trouble with the wing commander. He was not even a radar man and had served many years in the ranks as a wireless operator.

No doubt I made a very poor job of concealing my opinion of him, but as an RAFVR officer with two rings I must have seemed terribly cocky towards a regular airman

216

with three rings, and he was always calling me into his office to put me in my place. When he moved into our mess at 24 Castle Street, he took over for himself the best bedroom and I was banished to a tiny servant's room at the back.

It was now over three years since I had left England and I still had another year to serve overseas. The rule for repatriation was three years for married men and four years for single, but I found out one day that service in certain commands, including Aden, with the worst climates would count towards earlier repatriation. I pursued this loophole through all the official channels to New Delhi, until I managed to establish that I would be "time expired" on October 22, having secured nine weeks' remission of sentence in respect of my months spent in Aden.

It was at long last possible to begin to think and dream of going home and one day of taking up life in England where I had left off more than three years before. So after taking advice from Percy Gaddis, I chose an honest dealer in gems and selected a large cornflower blue sapphire in his tiny boutique in a Colombo arcade. Together with six tiny white sapphires for a setting, since no diamonds could be obtained, I had this made up into a ring which I insured and committed to the registered post for its long journey home to England.

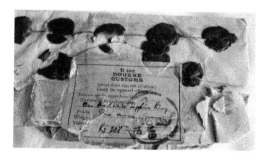

"I committed the ring by registered post"

Three times during the year I made the long journey to Delhi and back by air, for we were now firmly put in our place as just a part of the overall command. Our task in Ceylon was to form the southern part of a comprehensive radar system designed to protect Palk Strait, the waters between Ceylon and the tip of India, for that was destined to be the assembly location for a seaborne invasion of the Far East.

At least that was the story we were told, and accordingly I became involved in siting and commissioning both high- and low-flying stations in the extreme north of Jaffna, and in much liaison with New Delhi. It is difficult to appreciate just how unusual it was in 1944 to fly on a long journey, for there was no such thing as an airliner as we know it today. When I took off on my first journey to Delhi, on January 6, it was in an old Lockheed Hudson with no seats and no heating. The journey took two days, with stops at Cochin and Bangalore (overnight) and then Bombay, before the last perilous leg across the Ghats to New Delhi. We actually reached the height of 14,000 feet, shivering with cold in our khaki shorts, and then spiralled down into temperatures of 100-plus degrees to land at Palam. There were no toilets in transport aircraft, and if one of the two engines failed the outlook was gloomy indeed.

My journey back to Ceylon brought me a piece of luck, in the form of a telephone call from the transit officer to report to Palam at midnight. Here on the tarmac was a Lancaster bomber, the first four-engine aircraft to come to the east on a proving flight, and as soon as I had climbed aboard she thundered off into the night on a non-stop flight to Ceylon.

She was equipped with the new centimetric wavelength radar which effectively gave the pilot a map of the terrain in front of him, a system given the codename of H2S, which I found fascinating to watch. The last part of the trip I spent standing up in the astrodome to watch the first glimmerings of dawn light. The visibility was fantastic and I could pick out Adam's Peak, the sacred mountain of Lanka, at a distance of over 100 miles. Because of the visibility we had to divert from Colombo and land at Sigiriya, with the massive rock towering above the massive bomber.

April 26 was when the wartime postal service actually delivered my sapphire ring to Bere Regis in Dorset, where Peggy was teaching domestic science, so that date became the formal date of our engagement. By 9 am the whole school was buzzing with the news and our parents were informed by telephone. In fact the only person who did not know about it was me, for I was on another flying visit to New Delhi, and Peggy's cable only reached me five days later back in Colombo.

We continued to receive a visit from the Japanese on full-moon nights, although these were confined to the east coast. They seemed to be probing our radar system, but on one occasion a bomb was dropped uncomfortably close to our station at Kalkudah, and on another the single plot expanded into a mass of multiple echoes and we thought that we had either parachutists or gliders; but all that landed were strips of aluminium foil.

I had these analysed at Colombo University in case they were more sinister than they appeared, and then sent a full report to Delhi. This was the first recorded use by the Japanese of the system which the RAF in Europe had codenamed "Window", but of that we knew nothing at the time as it was still secret.

Troop reinforcements were coming in from England, and one day I found myself interviewing a set of radio operators, all miserable and dirty after weeks aboard a trooper.

"Name?"

"Romans, Sir."

"That's an odd name—you must be a mongrel relation of mine."

"Yes Sir. I'm your cousin."

And so it was I met my first cousin Derrick, whom I had last seen as an infant. It was my job to place these reinforcements and I exercised my discretion in sending Derrick to what I expected to be a permanent station in

Ceylon, instead of to some new little mobile units which we were training with a view to moving forward into Burma.

During these last few months of "waiting for the boat" I took advantage of any opportunities which the air force life afforded, playing rugby, soccer and hockey, even cricket. I joined the Royal Colombo Yacht Club and raced dinghies around the wrecks in Colombo Harbour, took part in two courts-martial and even applied for a permanent commission just in case I might need a job after the war.

Hockey team

Playing cricket

But above all I seized every opportunity to go flying, with the excuse of visiting stations all over the island to visit and inspect. Mostly I flew in Ansons.

***

On October 22, 1944 I was officially "time expired" and the daily index in my pocket diary which had started the year on January 1 at 295 had clocked itself down to zero. As proof that the air force actually regarded me as due to go home, I was formally posted from 183 Wing to Base HQ, Colombo, although I continued to live in the 183 Wing mess and indeed to go on working as usual. I did allow myself a little time off, however, to acquire a few things to take home such as bedsheets and other UK-unobtainable items.

On 30 October an official 222 signal gave authority for my repatriation, an occasion which gave rise to a fairly wild party in the mess in celebration of my good fortune. As a climax, some of my so-called friends thought it would be appropriate to push me out of the window, and against odds of some 25 to 1 I had little chance of effective resistance. Nevertheless, I put up a fight to the last moment and then, overbalancing on the sill, grabbed one of the lynch mob and took him out with me. Together we fell heavily on the gravel with me underneath.

At first I thought nothing was broken, but I soon found one finger hanging out of shape and beginning to hurt: I had broken a tendon and chipped a bone which had to be set in splints and plaster, but who cares? Not me—I was "on the boat" and on standby to embark on November 10.

Eleven days to go! Finger or no finger, I passed an easy weekend playing hockey and sailing, little knowing what a cruel fate was waiting for me on the Monday morning. Summoned to report to the wing commander, I cared not what reproof he had in mind for me. In just four days' time I should be on the water and out of his life forever—or so I thought.

I snapped to attention and whipped out a smart salute. "You wanted to see me, Sir?"

He looked up, his face even more lugubrious than usual, and waved a signal form at me. "You're not going. Your repatriation is cancelled."

Then, to do him justice, he did try to explain why these new orders had come from AHQ, India. It seemed that a general election was pending in Canada and that the Canadian government had promised that all RCAF personnel would be repatriated after only two years. As this would mean a severe shortage of radar personnel, AHQ would not let me go and so poor me became a solitary pawn in a power struggle between London and Ottawa.

It all seemed desperately unfair, so I took myself off to the Secretariat, the HQ of 222 Group, and somehow wangled my way in to see the SPSO, Group Captain Watson, and through him I progressed to the AOA, Air Commodore Richardson, who advised me to make a formal request "through the proper channels".

I was getting nowhere scaling the heights of the RAF Command, so I started in again at a lower level and found an ally in the legal department, in the shape of a squadron leader who was in civil life a barrister and moreover a Cockney and a Jew. He helped me to phrase and submit a petition for my case to be reconsidered and that seemed to me to be all I could do.

I had little heart to do any serious work now, but I continued to take every chance to travel about the island. The day after I should have been on the water, I drove all the way up to the extreme north of Jaffna peninsula to see the new MRU at Periyanaddutevanturai and stayed on for a few days in a tented camp which housed a field hospital. This had its own surgical specialist, and he broke and reset my hammer finger for me, this time setting it with a bend on the first joint so that the tendon on the end joint would have a better chance to heal—or so he said. (Today, as I write this 43 years later, it is still bent, but only a little bit, so perhaps he did me more good than harm.)

I hitched a lift back to the racecourse airstrip by air and next day was off again on another self-appointed holiday trip, this time going up country to Kandloya driving a large jeep. This was the first time I had been able to get my hands on one of these fabulous vehicles and I drove it flat out with the windscreen lowered. The resulting 60 mile an hour wind was a joy in the sweltering coastal area, but it got colder and colder as I climbed into the mountains and I contracted a streaming head cold.

December found me back in New Delhi, ostensibly to represent 183 Wing at a conference but from my point of view to lobby for my repatriation. My friend Clifford Austin was now on the staff at AHQ, and he looked after me well, but the most important thing for me was a virtual promise of a place on a troopship from Bombay in January, so I flew back to Colombo in high hopes, packed up all my kit and waited.

In these last days I began to look back on my three years in Ceylon with something akin to nostalgia. I had made many friends, most of whom I should never meet again and several who were already dead—from enemy action, from tropical illnesses, from flying and other accidents and from suicide. I had slow-marched to many gravesides and quick-marched away again, then sat for hours trying to write the letter to the widow or mother.

I had seen the fabulous beauty of the mountains and swum in the warmest of seas, sharks or no sharks. I had driven over every mile of paved road on the island in a great variety of vehicles and even used a dumper truck where no road existed. I had flown in many types of aircraft and then been reduced to the humble pedal cycle. I had taken part in two courts-martial and many impromptu parties. I had been praised by an admiral and censured by two group captains. I had learned many old RAF ballads and helped to write new ones applicable to "our" war.

It had all been rather fun, but any day now it would be just a memory.

Chapter 17

The Boat

I stood on the deck of the *Durban Castle* and looked back at the receding coast of Ceylon with mixed feelings. To be on the ship, bound for home, after more than four years away was too good to be true, and yet-it was the old "prisoner of war complex", that sudden feeling of needing to cling on to the prison you know in case you are moving to something worse.

Not for the first time in my service life, an abrupt signal from some disembodied HQ had suddenly separated me irrevocably from the friends and surroundings I had got to know, and now I had to start all over again. A mere 24 hours ago I had been going about my business in 183 Wing on the golf course when the order came to report for embarkation at Colombo Harbour at dawn on the morrow: back to number 24 Castle Street to pack the last of my small kit and don my last clean shirt and a pair of slacks for dinner, which I passed as unobtrusively as possible, not wanting any more broken fingers.

After the meal we were sitting quietly in the bar, with no thought of a party in mind, when some bright spark decided that the four who had gone off to play poker in the anteroom ought to be offered a drink to celebrate my departure. When they declined, he sent them in a drink anyway; that is to say, he tossed a few drops of the dregs from his glass over the openwork lattice at the top of the wall dividing the rooms.

Quite logically, they sent a reply of the same kind by the same route, but, as was to be expected, the drops landed not on the originator but on an innocent bystander (or rather innocent bar sitter). Well, good bars always have soda syphons and so the means of escalation was readily to hand.

One squirt led to another, and very soon I found myself caught up in a conflict like poor, neutral Belgium, trying to keep out of it but powerless to do so. Soon it became a free-for-all with ill-defined sides in the contest. In fact, the original teams seemed to amalgamate into a common, wet-shirted posse, bent on flushing out any dry-shirted lurkers from the other rooms and helping them not to miss the fun of getting soaked.

The natural successor to the soda water syphon is the fire bucket, and this has the advantage of being more readily rechargeable, so before long the stone floor of number 24 was ankle-deep in water, liberally mixed with sand, for who stops to read the label in a crisis?

When the battle was at its height my old Yatesbury colleague and friend, George Woollatt, now a squadron leader, walked in the door, immaculately dressed in his best khaki jacket, having come back from a recital of classical music. A whole bucketful of water took him full in the face, and he, too, had no recourse but to join in the fun. With a senior officer involved, a salute appropriate to his rank was needed, so out came the soda acid fire extinguishers, and after that a sort of truce was called for lack of ammunition.

As soon as I could, I sneaked away upstairs, to find my unloved commanding officer, not exactly hiding but certainly trying not to be seen and curiously deaf to the shouting and hubbub.

We met, eye to eye, said not a word, and I never saw him again, for at dawn I crept out of the sleeping mess to the waiting driver, with no goodbyes and no backward glances.

I shared a cabin with three other flight lieutenants, one of whom, Bill Bedford, was later to become the first pilot to fly the "Flying Bedstead" from which the Harrier V-TOL was developed. We made good progress to Egypt and through the Suez Canal and then stopped at Port Said for two whole weeks, because the extreme cold weather in England had delayed the shipping turnaround in all the British ports and we could not sail until the backlog was cleared, for it was highly dangerous to hang about in the North Atlantic and the last part of our journey would be made as fast as possible.

So we sat in the Suez and waited, with no shore leave for anyone. The only exception to this rule was a member of our cabin, who somehow wangled permission to go into Suez on the last night and came back hopelessly drunk—or so we thought—at midnight. Next morning, as we put to sea, he lay comatose in his bunk, accompanied by an empty bottle of Egyptian-made whisky and a couple of day-old chicks, probably acquired from a gully-gully man in some dockside bar.

But by the afternoon we became worried and shopped him to the MO, thereby saving his life, for, apart from a potentially lethal dose of gut rot, he had burst a stomach ulcer. That night we three reluctant cabin mates were roused from bed and made to report to the MO, for our patient had developed the DTs. It seems that he had jumped out of bed and run through the sick bay, trailing a length of tubing and a blood bottle still hooked into his leg and screamed that the ship was taken over by German spies.

At this, the sick berth attendant had fainted and so the MO made us take it in turns, sitting up all night to restrain the patient, by force if necessary. No doubt we helped to save his life, but no word of thanks did we ever get from the ungrateful misery. The MO had decided to put him off in Gibraltar, with which we heartily concurred for three occupants is a better number than four in a two-berth cabin, but as we put into the Rock the MO relented, for the case was an interesting one and he wanted to keep it to himself.

***

Now came the last leg of the journey—and the most dangerous—as we put out into the Atlantic under escort. Opinion was divided among the rumour-mongers as to whether we would go east or west of Ireland and whether to Liverpool or Glasgow—or maybe to the bottom, for there were clearly U-boats about. Escorting destroyers dashed everywhere, dropping depth charges and flashing signals, while overhead a relay of Sunderlands kept us company during the daylight hours.

When night fell, word was passed that all troops were to keep fully clothed all night, and the captain himself came on the Tannoy to reinforce this order. He could not conceal the anxiety in his voice, nor the weariness, and we needed no second telling. I knew we were well north of Ireland, for I made a simple sextant out of a sheet of paper folded diagonally (to give an exact 45 degrees) so that I could measure the altitude of Polaris and so determine our latitude. This same simple reference point enabled me to know when our average course became south of east and were therefore shaping to pass down the Irish Sea.

I awoke with a start after only a short while of fitful sleep and knew at once by the change in the throb of the engines that we were at a reduced speed. On deck, in the first grey light of the February dawn, I could make up a faint blueish smudge on the horizon to port—England! So began 36 hours of continuously mounting excitement as the coastline neared, then the channel buoys, the Liver building, the Prince's landing stage, the first warp snaking to the shore party, the sight of a British policeman and our last dinner on board.

Then, inevitably, a pause to reflect that we were still confined to ship; that although in a British port, it was still eight weeks since anyone had had any news from home, that all our families might be dead, killed by the flying bombs which were now striking the south. Might as well try and get some sleep. No chance!

A bang on the cabin door. "All officers to report in the lounge at once," and there we found the disembarkation

228

party and the friendly Customs officers to process us and hand out leave passes, railway warrants, train timetables and ration cards. I was through all this by two in the morning and went on deck to watch the baggage being hoisted ashore—and there, down below, was a red telephone box.

It was worth a try: down to A deck, find the gang plank, tell the armed guard I was supervising the baggage party, walk briskly through and ashore. Well, technically I was still afloat on a giant pontoon, but no matter …

Lift the receiver. "Number, please."

"Trunks." Click. Purr.

"Trunk call number, please."

"Gillingham Dorset 27."

"Insert three and fourpence."

Ping, ping, ping. Plop, plop, plop.

Various half-heard sounds told me that I was through to London, then Salisbury, then "Your number is ringing."

Purr, purr, purr. (This will give them a surprise!)

"Two, seven."

(Quick. Press button A) "Hello. It's me. Are you well?"

It was the first time for over four years that I had spoken, even by telephone, to my family, and I ran and skipped along the landing stage like a child. Sleep was almost impossible, but I forced myself to lie on my bunk for a while, waiting for the dawn.

A day to remember was February 21: the scramble to find all one's kit; the ride in a commandeered coal lorry; Lime Street Station: a scramble for a porter; a quick dash to the post office to send two telegrams; the crowded train taking hours to reach Euston; an hour's wait for a taxi; another scramble for a porter with a trolley; the strain on the faces of the Londoners; the abominable taste of the station buffet's scrambled egg made with dried egg powder; the queues at Waterloo; the same old 06.00 train; fast to Salisbury; the memories of Salisbury Station; the stopping stages across the plain and then the gathering speed off the plain into Blackmore Vale. I hung out of the window for a glimpse of Melbury and Dunclrffe Wood in the moonlight.

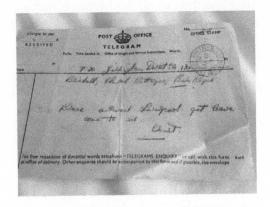

Telegram about Liverpool arrival

Meanwhile, that morning in Bere Regis, Peggy had received my telegram, secured seven days' leave and set off on her bicycle to cover the 25 miles to Gillingham. My first glimpse of her was as a solitary figure waiting on the dimly-lit down platform, just as my last glimpse had been on the up platform, only ten yards away but four years and two months ago. It was good to be back.

We were married by special licence six days later and the two old Misses Stadden, (whom I had once helped by harvesting their apple crop for them before the war) came to strew flower petals in our path as we walked from the church.

Bruce and Peggy's wedding day

The RAF soon claimed me back, and for a few more months Peggy had to continue her teaching post for it was illegal to leave her job under the Direction of Labour Act. I was posted to Broadstairs in Kent, but we used to snatch weekends together in London, staying anywhere the Salvation Army could find us a bed. The war in Europe was passing to its close, but the last-resort V1 and V2 weapons were doing much damage to London and the south.

The V2, in particular, was unnerving since it arrived supersonically and there was not even the familiar whine of a falling bomb to give you a few seconds' warning to dive under the table. Trains were overcrowded, and long queues were formed behind barriers away from the gates to the individual platforms. When finally the platform numbers

231

were announced, the queue broke as everyone rushed forward and that was the moment to get caught up in the turmoil and swept among the front runners. This called for an alert eye and perfect timing: it never failed to get me a seat.

But the war in Europe was not for me, and soon I was back in Yatesbury on yet another course, this time to bring me up to date with the new centimetre wavelengths—so that I could be sent back to the Far East, I suspected.

I was in Yatesbury when Germany surrendered, and we were given the day off, rather like an extra half-holiday at a school prizegiving. That day I cycled the 40 miles to Gillingham, played three sets of tennis and then cycled back to Yatesbury by midnight.

When I was posted to TRE at Malvern, we determined to set up some sort—any sort—of home together, and this we did in a strange assortment of boarding houses; but the fitting end of this tale lies in a tiny white tent by a stream in the middle of Exmoor.

I had secured some leave and scrounged a few gallons of petrol and together we discovered the Weir Water Valley. On a little crystal receiving set I had made, just powerful enough for a set of earphones, I heard the awesome news: the war was over, the atom bombing of Hiroshima and Nagasaki having forced a Japanese surrender. The early work of the Cavendish laboratory had borne its fruit and the world would never be the same again.

I sat for a while by the stream outside the tent and thought. I knew, far better than most people at the time, what the awful potential of atomic energy was, for good or evil—and now that the genie was out of the bottle, could he ever be put back?

Weir water

For the present, I thought, the results were wholly good, for those few thousands of Japanese just fried in Hiroshima had saved the lives of millions of their fellow countrymen and mine who would have died in a fight to the finish. And I had been spared from having to go out East again to take part.

For the future, what? Germany and Japan were all but destroyed, but what of a Russia who had actually signed a treaty with Hitler which enabled him to attack us? There was no answer at that time, and I stayed in grave doubt.

The answer came some months later, with the news that the now dreaded Russia had exploded her own bomb. I actually rejoiced, for here, at last, was a balance of power which meant that no country could hope to be the aggressor and win.

Writing now, forty years later in 1987, I can modestly claim to have been right; and so I say to my children and grandchildren:

Never forget what Hitler did to the Jews.

Never forget what the Japanese did to those they enslaved.

Never be afraid to defend yourself, or to fight for your life if need be.

Never forget that if I hadn't done my tiny little bit to help defeat the enemy, you wouldn't be here today.

Enjoy the peace you have known all your lives, but don't ever take it for granted.

Postscript

Bruce's daughter, Rosemary, at the site of the Chain Home Low station at Worth Matravers, Dorset, where the work of the scientists during the war is recognised

ing Source UK Ltd.
Keynes UK
V012208141120
06UK00002B/132